ALAMO
COLLEGES

NORTHWEST VISTA COLLEGE

Learning Resource Center
3535 N. Ellison Dr. ◆ San Antonio, TX 78251

JUMP-START YOUR ONLINE CLASSROOM

D1520215

JUMP-START YOUR ONLINE CLASSROOM

Mastering Five Challenges in Five Days

David S. Stein and Constance E. Wanstreet

STERLING, VIRGINIA

COPYRIGHT © 2017 BY
STYLUS PUBLISHING, LLC.

Published by Stylus Publishing, LLC.
22883 Quicksilver Drive
Sterling, Virginia 20166-2102

Library of Congress Cataloging-in-Publication Data

The CIP for this text has been applied for.

13-digit ISBN: 978-1-62036-580-9 (cloth)
13-digit ISBN: 978-1-62036-581-6 (paperback)
13-digit ISBN: 978-1-62036-582-3 (library networkable e-edition)
13-digit ISBN: 978-1-62036-583-0 (consumer e-edition)

Printed in the United States of America

All first editions printed on acid-free paper
that meets the American National Standards Institute
Z39-48 Standard.

Bulk Purchases

Quantity discounts are available for use in workshops and for
staff development.
Call 1-800-232-0223

First Edition, 2017

10   9   8   7   6   5   4   3   2   1

To the new online instructors who have enriched our research and practice

CONTENTS

How will I know my students if I cannot see their faces or hear their voices? How will I be able to read their nonverbal cues for understanding? What is it like to be at a distance from my students and not be with them in a physical classroom? Can I really teach online? Those are questions from new online instructors whom we have supported and instructed in meeting the challenges of online teaching. Perhaps you too have asked those same questions.

Online Opportunities

Every year more online or technology-enhanced learning experiences become part of the educational environment, and the number of students taking online courses on residential campuses continues to grow. The National Center for Educational Statistics (NCES, 2016) reports that 5.5 million distance education courses were offered in postsecondary institutions (27% of courses offered) with 2.8 million students (14% of total enrollments) taking at least one distance education course during fall 2013. The numbers for fall 2014 increased 3.7% over the previous year. In addition, 71% of chief academic leaders reported that online learning is critical to their long-term institutional success (Allen, Seaman, Poulin, & Straut, 2016). It is becoming clear that obtaining employment in higher education will be enhanced by possessing online teaching skills.

In addition to increased courses, new instructional tools are creating environments that are mobile, interactive, and collaborative. How these trends are influencing and changing the way instructors relate to learners and provide learning experiences presents new challenges to the online classroom.

Opportunities for online teaching are also associated with increasing employment for adjunct/part-time instructors, particularly in online universities. The NCES (2016) shows a 104% increase in part-time faculty between 1993 and 2013. Part-time faculty in the fall of 2013 accounted for about 40% of faculty positions (NCES, 2016).

Jump-Start Your Online Classroom: Mastering Five Challenges in Five Days presents immediate guidance on teaching tips, tools, and techniques for creating worthwhile and exciting learning experiences in a digital class-room. Making the transition from being physically present with your learn-ers to being in a virtual environment requires a commitment to a new way of thinking about instruction and the roles of learners and teachers and recog-nizing when the physical classroom space is necessary and when learning can be enhanced through online teaching tools and interactions.

Who Will Benefit From This Book?

This book is for new instructors, instructors contemplating the uses of the virtual classroom, and for those who support online teaching and wish to know more about it. The tips, tools, and techniques offered here will help you establish an instructional presence online and will prepare you to negoti-ate your way through the beginning weeks of your online course.

In this text, we address the practical issues of preparing yourself to teach online, examining the virtual classroom space, engaging with learners, and assessing learner performance in your virtual classroom. We show how to build an environment that is centered on the learners being actively engaged in solving problems, evaluating evidence, analyzing arguments, and reflect-ing on the learning experience. You will find guidance on teaching online, resources to provide additional information, and activities to help you plan, manage, and facilitate online instructions during the beginning weeks of your class.

As you read through the text, you will hear the voices of those who par-ticipate in online learning as well as those who are becoming first-time online instructors. Most texts about teaching are written by instructors who provide prescriptions for teaching. We have listened to our learners in a variety of online courses and present an online andragogy consistent with their voices.

How This Book Is Organized

After an introduction to the online environment, this book is organized around the immediate challenges you will face in teaching online. We work on everyday problems in teaching online and develop solutions informed by our shared experiences and text material. Each section of the book focuses on a particular challenge in becoming an online teacher. These chal-lenges include the following:

- Making the transition to online teaching
- Building online spaces for learning

- Preparing students for online learning
- Managing and facilitate the online classroom
- Assessing learner outcomes

First Challenge: Making the Transition to Online Teaching

In Chapter 2, "Are You Ready to Teach Online?" you will analyze your competencies as a beginning online instructor and learn how to overcome the physical separation of instructors and learners in the online environment.

In Chapter 3, "Addressing Concerns About Teaching Online," you will reassess how you conceptualize class time and examine your attitude toward online teaching.

In Chapter 4, "Thinking and Acting Like an Online Instructor," you will develop communication and time management plans as a professional development practice. This chapter also helps you establish an online persona and the trust that students will learn in a well-designed course.

Second Challenge: Building Online Spaces for Learning

Chapter 5, "Building Spaces and Places for Learning," features a discussion of public and private class spaces and the role they play in learning. You will also have the opportunity to assess various tools that may be appropriate for your course.

Third Challenge: Preparing Students for Online Learning

Creating connections is the theme of Chapter 6, "Preparing Your Students for Online Learning." You will learn how to compose a welcome message and assess various ways you and your students can learn about one another.

Fourth Challenge: Managing and Facilitating the Online Classroom

Chapter 7, "Managing and Facilitating the Online Classroom," contains practical ideas for promoting participation, increasing the effectiveness of discussions, and monitoring interactions. A case study that facilitates reflection on how to handle a frustrated student is included.

Fifth Challenge: Assessing Learner Outcomes

Chapter 8, "Assessing Learning in the Online Classroom," describes how to use authentic assessments and formulate feedback and provides tools learners can use to demonstrate competence.

Appendices

The appendices contain templates, checklists, and strategies that will help you meet the challenges you'll face during the first few weeks of your course. Two questionnaires provide insight into your preparation for and attitude toward online teaching. A template and checklist will help you develop your course communication and time management plans, and a list compiled by our former learners provides a base for you to explore technology tools that might be applicable for your course. To reduce development time, a sample welcome letter is provided along with instructions for developing a scavenger hunt to familiarize your students with your course management system. Case studies and suggestions developed by our former learners are also included.

Instructor Resources

Should you adopt this book for faculty development, visit your-online-classroom.com for the following resources:

- PowerPoint slides
- Welcome letter rubric
- Expectations message rubric
- Communication plan rubric
- Time management plan rubric
- Case study discussion guidance
- Suggested additional activities
  - Start Here activity checklist and rubric
  - Three interactive learning spaces checklist and rubric
  - Social presence activity checklist and rubric
  - Assessment activity checklist and rubric

Meet Teaching Challenges in Five Days

This book and supporting materials are designed to equip you with the competencies needed to meet the challenges of teaching online in five days. We recommend working on one challenge per day, beginning with the first challenge, and investing about four hours of your time daily. Your time will be allocated to reading and reflecting on content, working on practical activities to further support and reinforce your learning, and applying content to a course you are or will be teaching. Let's begin!

David S. Stein and Constance E. Wanstreet

I

THE ONLINE ENVIRONMENT

To teach online, I must make the commitment to build a learning environment in which learners and I feel safe to explore ideas, to comment frequently on those ideas, to be present in the space, and to contribute to the ongoing discourse. . . . Teaching an online course requires adequate preparation, clarity, and concern for your learners. It can be rewarding when done with caution.

—Tim, graduate teaching assistant

As a classroom teacher, one of my biggest struggles has always been taking a step back and letting students work things out. I'm definitely an extrovert who likes to help, and that can sometimes be counterintuitive. When I teach online, I need to remember this and avoid being too heavily involved in discussions, viewing myself as a moderator, facilitator, and clarifier rather than a lecturer.

—Sarah, new online instructor

Your process of becoming an online instructor involves how the following aspects of an online learning environment affect your teaching: social practices, tools, participants, learning community, and outcomes. Each of these elements influences your practices as an online instructor. After completing this chapter, you will be able to do the following:

- Explain social practices that help create an environment for learning
- Describe tools used to create private and public learning spaces
- Name ways to help learners feel connected to you and one another
- Identify ways to foster coownership of the teaching and learning process
- Describe the role of authentic assessments in measuring outcomes

Interactive, Collaborative Framework

The challenges you will face as a new online instructor mirror the characteristics of the environment where teaching and learning will take place. The use of electronic tools and the availability of information can foster

Figure 1.1. Elements of the online environment.

a learning environment that is highly interactive, collaborative, and constructivist. We envision online learning environments as having the following elements: social practices, tools, participants, learning in community, and outcomes. Figure 1.1 illustrates the components of the framework that reflect your immediate online teaching challenges (Stein & Wanstreet, 2011).

Social Practices

Social practices regulate actions and interactions within the online learning space. Instructors need to understand how learners interact with their digital devices and with one another. Faculty and instructional support staff help learners manage text-based and voice-based interactions to promote critical thought and deep learning. This involves skill in coaching discussion groups; providing feedback on the quality of online discussions; and offering guidance on expressing oneself online through text, emoticons, and other nonverbal communication.

As faculty change their mind-set from being the primary source of information to guiding students in critically selecting content, what faculty say will become less important than what they do to help generate critical thought. Learners can receive guidance instantly from international scholars, join teams of inquirers from around the world, and work on their academic journey anywhere. Learners are able to knit together formal and informal learning resources to complete an inquiry. How learners form their study teams and what the team learned about the inquiry can become more important than any single individual with whom learners study.

Tools

Instruction is shaped by the interaction of tools, learners, and the instructor. Tools include any device that mediates or shapes the instructional interaction, such as synchronous and asynchronous technology, books, online resources, group size, online learning theories, and self-concepts. Tools continually change, and in the process they change how we teach and learn. For example, new Internet technologies, social networking sites, wikis, and virtual environments extend learning environments beyond our time and space boundaries.

Participants

The participants in our online classrooms—faculty, learners, subject matter experts, and instructional support staff—each have roles in the learning process. In the online classroom, instructors focus on the learning process rather than on imparting their content knowledge. Learners build knowledge by bringing global content sources available anywhere on the Internet into the class to challenge instructors and one another. Experts and others in instructional support can provide immediate assistance and resources to aid learning. Instructors help learners manage this complex, media-rich environment by orchestrating multiple views and helping learners make new meanings.

Insights From a New Online Instructor

The truth is when you work with other people, work will rarely be divided fairly. We will have some members who do not contribute, some who take control over the whole project, and some who do their fair share. These are the traits of different people. I have been in many groups where I have felt like one other member and I did all of the work. I have also been in groups where I tried to contribute but another member really did not allow it. There will be a learning experience one way or another. I feel the trick is for the instructor to monitor and provide feedback. Also, there should be a clear function for each member. We need to observe our students closely and give them the best tools we can to be successful.

Learning in Community

Ideally, learning takes place in academic communities whose members recognize that learners are coproducers of knowledge. These communities are based on the idea that social groupings can facilitate individual and collective learning. Learning in community means acquiring new basic skills, including the ability to work in groups with people of various backgrounds; to communicate effectively, orally and in writing; to combine independent and interdependent work to produce a meaningful outcome; and to use social networking and collaborative software.

Learning in community means being engaged in the task of knowledge building rather than knowledge acquisition and retention. Even in courses that emphasize individual knowledge acquisition, the instructor, at a minimum, becomes part of the student's learning community.

Outcomes

Outcomes are the target of the learning activity. Outcomes refer to the problem space where activity is directed. An example might be the problem of changing a traditional course into a Web-based course. The problem is shaped or transformed into outcomes with the help of mediating instruments, tools, and signs. Yesterday, courses were focused on content dissemination and acquisition decontextualized from the daily lives of the learners. Today, courses are sets of knowledge demonstrations. Instruction helps students connect their experience of learning to real-world applications. Faculty and learners alike assess and monitor the validity of content from multiple channels to achieve learning outcomes. In an online course, for example, the course website with its discussion board, chat room, e-mail, and other tools of technology are used by the instructor and by learners to produce course outcomes, such as research, presentations, projects, or papers.

The interaction among tools, participants, social practices, community, and the outcome creates an environment for a meaningful online educational experience.

Relating Online Elements to the Five Challenges

The aspects of the online environment provide a framework for addressing the five challenges that new online instructors face.

1. Making the transition to online teaching is a challenge based in social practices, which include establishing your presence through e-mail, discussion posts, and feedback. Communication processes are more sensitive online and can be easily misunderstood, which makes it imperative for you to model appropriate practice. Preparing a course calendar that lists the due dates for assignments is another practice that aids your learners in

adjusting to an online environment. Your words and actions, including the times of day you are online each week, help you establish your online persona and create an environment for learning.

2. The challenge of building online spaces for learning may be viewed through the tools available to you. Weekly spaces for direction, content, and the context for learning are fairly standard tools, as are community spaces on discussion boards for questions for the instructor and break rooms for nonacademic talk. Spaces may also include private areas for learners to record their emerging ideas and shared spaces for learners to negotiate meaning.

3. Preparing learners for online learning may be viewed through the perspective of the participants, who will need to feel connected to you and one another. Give your learners an opportunity to learn about you and each other. Preparing learners includes providing them with the syllabus, policies, procedures, expectations, and an opportunity to pose questions and concerns as well as with opportunities to explore the course site before the start of the class.

4. Learning in community provides a framework for the challenge of managing and facilitating the online classroom. Community provides a powerful context for learning where the members interact with one another in a meaningful way and accept coownership of the teaching and learning process. This includes, for example, moving discussions to higher levels by clarifying, expanding on content, explaining, critiquing content, and respectfully pushing others to see the assumptions behind their statements.

5. The assessment challenge is rooted in the learning outcome. Authentic assessments based on a combination of academic content and real-world problems reflect the course or unit outcome. Meaningful, timely feedback that addresses the strengths as well as areas of improvement promotes the outcome.

Challenges and Completion Plan

A number of reflection activities throughout this book are designed to help you meet the initial challenges you will face as a new online instructor. The challenges and completion plan in Table 1.1 will help you manage your progress in designing a schedule to accomplish each challenge. Indicate when you intend to complete each challenge. Mark the date completed as a record of your accomplishments.

TABLE 1.1

Challenges and Completion Plan

Element of the Online Environment Challenge	Activity	Suggested Due Date	Your Intended Completion Date
Social practices: Making the transition to online teaching			
	Complete Chapters 2, 3, and 4 reflection activities: • Complete the Beginning Online Instructor Competencies Questionnaire in Appendix A. • Complete the Attitude Toward Online Teaching Questionnaire in Appendix B. • Develop communication and time management plans for working on your course with resources in Appendices C, D, and E.	Day 1 11:59 p.m.	
Tools: Building online spaces for learning			
	Complete Chapter 5 reflection activity: • Explore technology tools (some are listed in Appendix F) and assess the extent to which they promote learning in your course.	Day 2 11:59 p.m.	
Participants: Preparing students for online learning			
	Complete Chapter 6 reflection activities: • Draft a course welcome letter and expectations message (samples are in Appendix G). • Read and reflect on How to Develop a Scavenger Hunt in Appendix H.	Day 3 11:59 p.m.	
Learning community: Managing and facilitating the online classroom			
	Complete Chapter 7 reflection activity: • Read and reflect on the Case of the Disgruntled Student.	Day 4 11:59 p.m.	

(*Continues*)

TABLE 1.1 (*Continued*)

Element of the Online Environment Challenge	Activity	Suggested Due Date	Your Intended Completion Date
Outcome: Assessing learner outcomes			
	Complete Chapter 8 reflection activities: • Read and reflect on the pastor's e-mail message about his late assignment. • Reflect on technology tools and the type of assessments that can help build confidence.	Day 5 11:59 p.m.	

Points to Remember

- Social practices help you establish your online persona and create an environment for learning.
- Use tools to build private areas for learners to record their emerging ideas and shared spaces for learners to negotiate meaning.
- Give your learners opportunities to feel connected to you and one another.
- Learning communities provide a powerful context for learning where the members interact with one another in a meaningful way and accept coownership of the teaching and learning process.
- Measure outcomes through authentic assessments and timely, meaningful feedback.

For Reflection

1. Examine Table 1.1: Challenges and Completion Plan.
2. Adopt or adapt the completion plan to your schedule.

FIRST CHALLENGE

MAKING THE TRANSITION TO ONLINE TEACHING

2

ARE YOU READY TO TEACH ONLINE?

I took an online course but it was not a good experience really. The professor never commented on my assignments. . . . I ended up passing, but barely. So I was really turned off on distance classes. There was no communication.

—Kathy, new online instructor

You have more opportunity for interaction with your instructor. I think I've learned more. I read a lot more. I get a lot more done. I have to focus a lot more because you're not in the classroom environment where, if you're not paying attention, you can always ask somebody. You've got to really get in there and dig it out yourself, so I feel I learn a lot more! A metaphor would be the difference between fast food (face-to-face) and something you have to prepare yourself (online). It's like the difference between a hamburger and a $40 steak. Online learning is not just thrown out there prepackaged.

—Rob, new online instructor

L earners, like instructors, have strong feelings about teaching and learning from a distance and are particularly concerned about online teaching. Teaching adults online incorporates adult and distance learning theories and is a skill that requires frequent communication among the members of the learning group. Online learning can be used for the transmission of information on an individual basis and can be efficient in providing content to those who have the ability to dig it out; in other words, self-directed learners.

However, online learning in our opinion is best used when the learners and instructor come together to understand the content deeply and to produce new understandings rather than simply rework present understandings. Fish and Wickersham (2009) characterize online learning as the cultivation of relationships between learners and instructor through frequent and meaningful communication. To teach online, an instructor must make the commitment to build a learning environment in which learners and the instructor feel safe to explore ideas, comment frequently on those ideas, be present in the space, and contribute to the ongoing discourse. This is a change perhaps in the social practices used in traditional higher education instruction.

In this chapter, we discuss and reflect on the transition from teaching in a physical space to teaching in a virtual classroom. After completing this chapter, you will be able to do the following:

- Describe ways to overcome the physical separation of instructors and learners online
- Explore the role of online presence
- Identify differences in communication processes online versus in person
- Analyze your competencies as a beginning online instructor

The Emerging Online Classroom

The emerging virtual classroom does not have walls, fixed boundaries, or a set time for instruction, nor is there a separation between the time for learning and the time for living. In this century, learning is electric, moving as fast as the Internet can carry the signal. We can reach our learners any time and from any place. Teaching and learning are mobile. Our learners can connect with us and with anyone who has the resources to enable learning to take place. We are moving from c-learning in the classroom to e-learning electronically to m-learning on mobile devices and beyond. Our classroom is the Web, and it is worldwide, rapid, exciting, and electric.

In this book we use the term *e-learning*, defined as "electronically mediated asynchronous and synchronous communication for the purpose of constructing and confirming knowledge" (Garrison, 2011, p. 2). The key to the definition is that learning is the process of taking information and integrating that information with information previously acquired to build a new thought and a greater understanding that had not previously existed among a group of learners.

E-learning, as we envision it, is learning that happens across time and space within and across communities of learners who come together for the purpose of improving their individual and mutual understanding. E-learning is the task of the participant; e-teaching is the task of the instructor as well as the shared practice of learners. The *e* represents more than simply electronic delivery; it represents the benefits of teaching online, including excitement, experience, exploration, and effectiveness as you see thought processes unfold.

What Is e-Teaching?

E-teaching presents the content, processes, and activities that bring about the construction of greater understandings. Our challenge in teaching online is to overcome the physical separation of ourselves from our learners and to integrate the act of teaching with the act of learning, acts that may be separated in time and space in the networked classroom. Of course, even in the physical classroom, the teaching act and the learning act may also be separated. An example is lecturing for a class period without any interaction between the instructor and learner, learner and learner, or learner and content. Perhaps in face-to-face classrooms we can see whether learning is happening, whereas in online classrooms, we must come to hear and read the learning.

Teaching in a virtual classroom is developing relationships with learners, content, tools, activities, and outcomes. Although some of you may have experienced the teaching act in a physical classroom or location, in this chapter we consider the ecology of the virtual classroom and how it may differ from being in a physical space. We focus on how our images of instruction and of a learning space influence the learning process.

Is e-Teaching Really Different?

Instructional values, skills, techniques, and style will come to define your practice of online teaching. To become a really good teacher, it is not enough to love to teach. You have to practice, reflect on your practice, and continually improve your practice. You have to be aware of your practice and how the tools for teaching and learning may change how we teach and how we learn. Although good teaching might be said to be the same across environments, how we act in a virtual classroom space is different. In the following, we discuss some of the ways environments differ.

Typically in an online classroom, members of the class may post thoughts and comments throughout the week or designated time period. Rather than having an assigned time to meet, class meets all week long. The class is always on (in session), and your presence goes beyond a single class meeting.

With online teaching, we come to know our students through their work products. Their voices and personalities are present in their postings, projects, and proposals. We may not ever see the faces of our students. We have to learn to listen to their words and see their thoughts emerge from the dialogue.

Our ability to present content is restricted by the spaces available in an online instructional platform or by good design practices for laying out material. In a virtual classroom, content is everywhere, including in the mind of the instructor. The instructor is not the sole source of content in a learning encounter. Information is instantly accessible and available to every learner at the moment it is needed. Instructor input can be challenged and argued with evidence from scholarly sources immediately available.

The virtual classroom is inclusive and diverse. You will find that virtual classrooms are diverse in terms of age, culture, and ethnicity. In the past, educators who taught at a distance used technology to bring about educational social justice, a realignment of society's educational resources to benefit those marginalized by race, class, and economic status, and those who were excluded because of age, job demands, or other life circumstances. The Internet and assistive technologies have increased the enrollment of those nontraditional learners who may have been left behind in educational attainment.

Time is flexible in the online classroom. Time zones become very important to instructors. Scheduling a face-to-face meeting online can be problematic when learners are in different cities, time zones, and countries. Learners can join the classroom from anywhere and can be involved in multiple activities. Instruction might be discontinuous and conducted over more than a single setting.

Communication processes are more sensitive and can be easily misunderstood. Feedback on work products that might seem constructive in person can easily be misinterpreted because of the lack of verbal and nonverbal cues. Learners want to know their work is being received and acknowledged. Instructors need to be present and show their presence through e-mail, discussion posts, and feedback through electronic or other means.

Insights From a New Online Instructor

Because there is a great amount of distance between students and teachers, communication is key. . . . Teachers have to take more time to help foster relationships because there are fewer opportunities for it to happen naturally. . . . The online format is, in some ways, no different from a traditional classroom. Information is shared, assignments are completed, and discussion is heard. Students also have the ability to create relationships and have their voices heard.

Online Instructor Competencies

We now turn to the competencies suggested for online instructors. The International Board of Standards for Training Performance and Instruction (2010) defined *competency* as the possession of a set of related knowledge, skills, and dispositions (attitudes) so one can perform the activities of an online instructor at the level expected by the professional community. This means that a competent online instructor has a deep understanding of the practices involved in teaching online and can apply the skills and knowledge in a variety of electronic teaching situations.

Many different frameworks exist for organizing the competencies for becoming an online instructor. Lee and Hirumi (2004) identified the following areas of performance that continue to be relevant:

- Interaction is made up of the skills of guiding and maintaining an interactive discussion, providing timely and constructive feedback, encouraging peer learning.
- Course management includes monitoring and assessing learner performance, facilitating presentations, locating support services.
- Course organization means developing expectations, objectives, and outcomes; linking content with activities and objectives; accounting for learning styles; and incorporating engaging activities.
- Use of technology suggests that the instructor can model the use of technology and follow best practices in online teaching.
- Content knowledge includes being current in the concepts, literature, and methods of the field of study.
- Teamwork skills are exhibited by the instructor in interactions with information technology and instructional design support teams.

Our framework for online teaching acknowledges Lee and Hirumi's (2004) performance areas in the context of the five challenges new online instructors face.

First Challenge: Making the Transition to Online Teaching

This challenge relates to Lee and Hirumi's (2004) performance area of course organization. Preparing yourself for online teaching means getting yourself mentally ready to adjust your teaching style. Perhaps your philosophy of instruction will need to be examined. You may need to adjust how you think about your relationship with learners, how the work of learning occurs, and how your role as instructor, the person responsible for building a learning environment, may change. In this stage you make the decision to teach or not to teach online, if you have the choice.

Second Challenge: Building Online Spaces for Learning

This challenge involves Lee and Hirumi's (2004) performance area of the use of technology and teamwork skills. Selecting appropriate tools and learning spaces means investing time in learning new technologies and deciding on the mode of instruction, whether synchronous, asynchronous, blended, or flipped, and the various permutations of combining text, audio, and physical and virtual spaces. You will also need to become familiar with your course management system as well as the tools for engaging learners and presenting content.

Third Challenge: Preparing Students for Online Learning

Interaction is the third of Lee and Hirumi's (2004) performance areas. Preparing learners for online learning recognizes that you as the instructor have to know the capabilities of your students, help build a welcoming environment, let your learners know how and when you are available, and set expectations for your learners as online participants.

Fourth Challenge: Managing and Facilitating the Online Classroom

Lee and Hirumi's (2004) performance area of course management relates to the fourth challenge. Facilitating online learning is the heart of teaching online. In this competency, you must manage but not control the teaching and learning processes, deal with issues of appropriate participation and engagement, find a balance between being present and being too present, and continually monitor and revise the course as conditions change. You will also need to know how to build a community that is cohesive and that supports individual and group learning.

Fifth Challenge: Assessing Learner Outcomes

Finally, we discuss Lee and Hirumi's (2004) performance area of content knowledge. Knowing the current concepts, literature, and methods in your field means you are able to communicate the standards for acceptable performance and provide timely, corrective, supportive, informational, and confirming feedback. In this competency, you will also need to know how to use the tools in your online instructional platform for testing, if that is a requirement for your course.

Thoughts About Good Instructional Practice

You may have noticed that many of the competencies would be considered good practice in a face-to-face classroom. We believe that good instructional practices do not vary according to the site of instruction; however, how we adapt and modify the practice is influenced by the environment for instruction. Zang and Walls (2009) found that commonly adopted practices included knowing students by name, asking students to discuss key concepts with learners from diverse backgrounds, providing experiences from students' daily lives to support content, and clearly communicating expectations for the timely submission of assignments. Although instructors emphasized giving prompt feedback, communicating high expectations, and time on task, encouraging cooperation among students was not as highly rated. However, we encourage cooperation among learners and using diverse talents of the learners to increase knowledge building. Today, the tools for cooperation and collaboration are more highly developed than they were at the time of Zang and Walls's study.

The online classroom is an exciting place where we are challenged to develop a relationship with our students without perhaps ever meeting our students in person. Our online competencies signal who we are, how we want to be seen, and how confident we are in an online environment. Students know us only through the way we use online spaces. A student once remarked to us regarding the personality of an instructor known to her only through the computer that

> her personality comes through all the time. I could tell you what type of personality she was before I ever saw her. A lot of times we benefit from hand gestures and eye contact, but with her she made it on e-mails, chats, and the telephone.

Points to Remember

- The challenge in e-teaching is to overcome the physical separation of ourselves from our students.
- Online classes meet all week long; your presence goes beyond a single class meeting.
- Communication processes are more sensitive online and can be easily misunderstood.
- Show your presence through e-mail, discussion posts, and feedback.
- Competencies for good online instruction are also good practices for face-to-face instruction.

For Reflection

1. Complete the Beginning Online Instructor Competencies Questionnaire in Appendix A.
2. What does the inventory tell you about the skills and knowledge you need to develop to become an excellent online instructor? Consider the following reflection questions:
   a. In which of the areas do you have strong experiential and conceptual knowledge?
   b. Which areas and which indicators signal a need for additional development?
3. Write a statement for increasing indicators rated 0 or 1 to a rating of 3.

3

ADDRESSING CONCERNS ABOUT TEACHING ONLINE

I realized that I needed to be prepared in terms of being able to communicate my thoughts well in a chat room setting with my group. If you have only a few lines to write, you need to be able to express yourself well. I also think instructors who have never taught online (or taken a class online) may be unsure of how to reach students through an online setting or even how to set up an online class.

—Lauren, beginning online teacher

I am wary of the "emotional" transition from in-person teaching to online teaching. Personally, I count on the reactions of my students to gauge how the course is going. I also feel like jokes, smiles, etc., are an important part of teaching. Trying to transition this human element into the online course will be challenging for me.

—Beth, beginning online teacher

Imagine: Your department chair approaches you and says, "Pat, I would like you to teach your first course online. Now your students will be able to participate in educational opportunities from any location."

You are thinking, "Wow! How do I begin thinking about what it might be like to teach online? How will I communicate with learners across time and space? How will I really get to know the learners?"

In this chapter we discuss five big concerns you might have as you prepare yourself to teach online. To teach online, an instructor must make the commitment to build a learning environment where learners and the instructor feel safe to explore ideas, comment frequently on those ideas, be present in the space, and contribute to the ongoing discourse. After completing this chapter, you will be able to do the following:

- Examine your teaching philosophy and your attitude toward online teaching
- Explore your online instructional platform for spaces that encourage interaction

- Reassess how you conceptualize class time
- Explain the function of a course plan
- Prepare a course calendar

Your Philosophy of Online Instruction

Your concerns about teaching online and how to address them are rooted in your philosophy of online instruction. Now is the time to formulate your philosophy if you haven't already done so. Levine (2007) suggests addressing five responsibilities in developing a philosophy of online teaching:

1. Become skilled in identifying the factors that contribute to success in learning.
2. Be consistent in your approach to teaching and consistently keep up with our fields.
3. Remember that what is taught in the classroom takes time to become real to learners.
4. Remember that learning is a dynamic process that may change daily.
5. Create an environment where learners feel safe and respected.

Our philosophy addresses how we value the following components of an online environment:

- Interactions that foster learning
- Our roles and responsibilities in creating a climate that encourages learners to seek knowledge and succeed in their learning endeavors
- Proficiency in facilitating collaborative learning
- The importance of helping learners take responsibility for their learning
- The importance of a quest for knowledge building

Our philosophy includes the following premises for teaching adults:

- Adults come to the classroom with the capacity to do the work. The capacity to do the work comes from prior learning and experiences.
- Adults learn when fully engaged cognitively, emotionally, and physically. Thoughts, feelings, and actions are part of every teaching transaction.
- Adults are accountable for their own learning. As teachers, we can build an environment for learning, we can create activities for learning, and we can provide information for learning; but it is the learner who makes the learning happen. Adults do the work of knowledge building. Teachers prepare, present, and evaluate the learning.

Knowledge Building

To guide your thoughts about developing a philosophy of online instruction, we include our insights about the importance of knowledge building. Learning in online environments can be viewed as a continuum ranging from individual information acquisition to collaborative knowledge generation, or adding to the existing body of content in a given field. On this continuum, learning is assessed either within an individual, a group, or a community of knowledge builders. Knowledge building is based on the idea that social groupings can facilitate individual and collective learning. In that way, knowledge building adds to the communal way of seeing the world, whereas learning adds only to an individual's repertoire of perspectives (Lipponen, 2000). Knowledge building has been described as a higher level of engagement and intellectual development achievable through online learning environments (McConnell, 2006).

Knowledge building moves learners to the center of the learning process. In online environments, a knowledge-building approach to learning resembles the way knowledge is created in the natural world. The goal is to expand on the existing canon, that is, the text and lectures, to solve problems through a collaborative process that improves on what is known about a subject. The learning involves making a contribution to understanding for all not just for some or for an individual (McConnell, 2006). New knowledge is generated through collaborative exchanges in which learners explore, test, and refine ideas held in public and private. Knowledge construction is the outcome—not a paper, exam, or project that addresses known content. A knowledge-building approach is appropriate when the subject matter is issue or problem focused rather than foundational.

Our philosophy of online instruction is informed by the importance of knowledge building and the premise that adults are capable of doing this work. In the context of our philosophy, then, we consider common concerns about teaching online.

First Concern: Where Is the Virtual Classroom?

The first concern is the location of the virtual classroom. The learning space for an online instructor is often shaped by the tools available in an online instructional platform that is designed to resemble the typical classroom and provide different levels of interactivity. Although various terms are used to describe where online instruction takes place, we use *online instructional platform* to differentiate the virtual learning space from a learning management system, which is based on a particular learning theory and philosophical approach to instruction, or a course management system, which is a collection of tools without an underlying learning theory (Glassman, 2016). The different online platforms provide different tools and different degrees of freedom for instructors to implement a particular approach to instruction, ranging from dependent learning to collaborative, interdependent learning.

Your organization may have purchased a system such as Blackboard, Canvas, or Desire to Learn, or perhaps your organization has designed its own system using platforms such as Moodle or other open-courseware systems. Tour the system and review the spaces that are available for posting content and encouraging interaction among the learners. Become aware of the limitations and advantages of your online instructional platform. The spaces will help you think about the types of learning activities that would enable students to work with each other, you, and the content and show how their individual thoughts are coming together to build a shared understanding of the issues presented.

One of the major advantages of online learning is that with careful construction of learning activities, we can see the learning happen. Every click leaves a trail. We can see the thoughts developing. We can see the struggles, and we can see the steps involved in addressing the learning task. We can see how long individuals work on their postings and the number of replies to the number of different learners. We can see the interactions.

Learning management, or course management, systems resemble the typical classroom. The instructor can post content (i.e., the lecture) in the form of a PowerPoint program with narration to demonstrate processes and procedures. With screen-capture software, it is easy to include voice and motion and to illustrate the steps in how do to something. Screencast-O-Matic (screencast-o-matic.com) is a free tool that allows you to easily display your screen and add voice and video so that learners can hear and see your instructions. Lecture-capture tools include MediaSite (www.sonicfoundry.com/mediasite) and Tegrity (www.mheducation.com/highered/platforms/tegrity.html).

An online instructional platform provides spaces for chats and large- and small-group discussion spaces, as well as repositories for storing readings, student work, and instructor resources. Anything that one might do in the physical classroom one can do in the electronic learning space. However, in the electronic learning space, time is different, and the spatial arrangements between the participants and the instructor are different.

Second Concern: How Is Time Different?

The second concern is time. In the physical classroom, the instructor controls the pace of instruction, the portion of the day allocated to the subject matter, and the time allocated to learner-to-learner and learner-to-instructor interactions. The teaching act (disseminating information) and the learning act (the acquisition of information and involvement with the content materials and activities) are synchronous, conducted in real time.

Synchronous teaching is defined as a real-time learning encounter in which learners, instructors, content, and technology come together in a single place for the purpose of instruction. Chats, video conferences, and Web conferences are examples of synchronous learning. Synchronous presentations require the learners to be online at the same time, similar to coming to a physical classroom. The difference is that learners in a synchronous environment can be located in different physical places.

E-time, which we are defining as teaching and learning events that occur at different times and do not require learners to be online at the same time, is indicative of asynchronous teaching and presents a different view of the online learning space. E-time signals shared control over the time of learning with the learner having greater control over the timing of the teaching and learning event. Engagement with content, instructors, and other learners occurs any time of day or evening (within the parameters established by the instructor). For example, an online discussion may take place during a 24-hour or longer time period.

E-time fits the learner's study rhythms. As one learner mentioned, she enjoyed asynchronous classes because she did not have to get up in the mornings and could work on the class when she was wide awake at 2:00 a.m. Online learning is significantly more convenient than its on-site equivalent. Instructors are able to pursue academic opportunities that require travel while still teaching the course and are relieved of some of the burdens of balancing child rearing and a career in the academy. Likewise, educational opportunities become available to adults who may be working a full-time job with inconvenient hours, may have family or child care commitments, or may have disabilities that profoundly limit their mobility.

Time can also be thought of as being constant in the online space. Unlike a physical classroom, an asynchronous classroom with discussion boards can be thought of as being always on, or in session. Class time occurs in 24-hour days rather than a few hours per week. How will you as an instructor be present in an anytime, anyplace learning space? How will you allocate time to share content, post your thoughts, provide feedback, post announcements, assess student performance, and hold office hours? Again, unlike a physical space, your learners may be in different time zones and will have expectations for the instructor's presence. For example, a learner in our fully online asynchronous course mentions the mutual responsibilities and obligations of students and the instructor to stay in touch in the following comment:

In an age when e-mail is connected to smartphones and most computers can use video conferencing technology, communication does not necessarily have to be delayed that much. Also, when the need arises, a conference over Google Hangouts or Skype can offer many of the benefits of an in-person meeting. I believe communication is the most important part of an online class. Two-way communication must always be present in any class. The instructor needs to be held accountable to provide all the adequate materials and clear instructions on assignments. In return, the students must ask questions and provide feedback when more clarity is needed. If these two do not communicate (in an online or a face-to-face class), neither side will be successful.

Boettcher and Conrad (2016) recommend that an online instructor should be present throughout the week and perhaps even daily. In our experience, learners want to know that you are there on a predictable basis. We recommend at least three times per week (if a module lasts one week) at a minimum in the discussion room sharing ideas, suggesting resources, and posing questions to raise the level of cognitive thought. Just a few minutes every day shows the learners that you are involved in the activity, reading posts, and, at the very least, monitoring the ways students engage with each other, the content, and the instructor. During a typical week, in addition to responding to discussion posts, we send feedback to individual students about the quality of their posts, respond to individual questions, check in on learners with late assignments or whose discussion responses could be improved, use the news feature to post more resources and readings, revise the next module, check links, and add new discussion threads as new issues are presented by the class.

In the beginning of the course, you may need to spend more time modeling appropriate ways to interact online. Online learning for many learners is not meant to be an independent study experience. The amount of guidance needed from the instructor will vary as the course intensifies and as the learners become more interdependent. A colleague suggests developing a daily schedule with instructor activities listed throughout the week (see Table 3.1).

Insights From a New Online Instructor

Prior to releasing the course I check for administrative concerns such as working links and typographical errors. I review the instructions. I check for questions for the instructor daily. On Days 1 through 3, I read and respond to threads; on Days 4 through 6, I provide group and individual feedback; on Day 6, I post an announcement of the upcoming lesson; and on Day 7, I post summaries and grades.

TABLE 3.1
Suggested Activities

Task	When to Complete	Notes
1. Review the course.	Two weeks before course opens	Review the content, learning goals, assignments, working links visibility for learners.
2. Review tools.	Two weeks before course opens	Test any digital tools learners will be using.
3. Participate in discussion.	Weekly	Monitor and participate in discussion threads. Suggest and post additional resources.
4. Monitor learner participation.	Weekly	Identify and contact participants who have not initiated contact by midweek.
5. Provide feedback.	Weekly	Provide individual and group feedback.
6. Grade assignments.	48 hours after due date	Grade all discussions and assignments.
7. Post grades.	48 hours after due date	Enter grades into the grade book.
8. Announce upcoming module.	Day before module opens	Post summaries and announcement of the upcoming module.

Third Concern: How Is Space Different?

A third concern is building teaching spaces and using space in an online classroom. A physical classroom space can be redesigned to accommodate different activities, such as large-group presentations, small-group activities, quiet spaces for self-directed tasks, and spaces to accommodate resources. Although it is possible to have multiple activities in a single place, most likely activities will be conducted sequentially, and how each space will be used is determined by the instructor.

Teaching primarily happens in the physical classroom space, and unless time is allocated for performance of tasks and reflection, it may be difficult to determine if learning is happening. In the physical classroom, instructors have said that nonverbal cues, which are absent in an online environment, can tell us if learning is occurring. Learning is an intellectual activity that we can observe only through performance. It is ongoing and should be distinguished from the acquisition of content. As online instructors, we learn how to see the learning happen through the texts that learners create. We see the learning through written expressions and hear the learning through other forms of mediated expressions. Because not being able to see learner reactions in real time is a concern of new instructors, we suggest encouraging learners to use punctuation marks and emoticons to communicate feelings and attitudes about the content and activities. Practice listening with your eyes. Picture the learner and listen for the rhythm and pacing in the text. Is the post constructed with detail? With source material? With care? Ask yourself, What are the learners telling me about their attitudes toward this assignment?

Our learners have told us that online learning does foster relationship development and that tools are available for seeing and hearing learners. For example, cohesiveness and a team mentality can be developed through instructor and student introductions, discussion posts, peer reviews, and group work. The instructor normally makes the initial introduction with a welcome message and encourages communication by way of classmate self-introduction posts. Through in-depth weekly posts and critical thinking, the instructor and students gain insight into the opinions and personalities of one another.

If you prefer face-to-face interactions, Google Hangouts, GoToMeeting, and Skype allow verbal and visual communication. Some students believe that relationships are deeper and more easily developed through digital communication. This type of communication can contribute to better cohesion and collaboration among students.

In the online classroom, spaces are also available to accomplish different intellectual activities. Unlike in the physical classroom, teaching and learning acts can occur concurrently and in a sequence often determined by the learner (unless the instructor blocks or hides certain activities until prerequisites are met). Teaching takes place in content pages and in the learner-controlled portions of a course, such as the discussion boards, collaborative workspaces, and e-mail messages. Learning happens at different times and in different spaces. In addition, learning happens online and offline throughout the week. Learners can return to discussion boards and other spaces set up for collaborative activities.

Insights From a New Online Instructor

The teaching happens through the lessons and activities; the learning, however, happens in the offline environment where the participants can reflect, develop their responses, gather any additional inputs, review their responses, and—when ready—return online to contribute. The discussion space is where much of the engagement takes place, through the use of required postings and responses. As the participants re-engage, their learning is enhanced by viewing the responses from their peers and incorporating that into their own understanding.

Fourth Concern: How Do I Manage the Presentation of Content?

A fourth concern of new online instructors is content management. Concerns revolve around the location of content, the use of technology, and how content is presented. Presentation of content is a function of how you believe learning occurs, the level of learning required in the course, the technologies available, and the ease of using certain technologies. In a knowledge-building environment, we move learners from being dependent to being independent to being interdependent.

We strongly support the premise that effective course delivery and content should be based on sound learning theory. How you deliver content and use technology influences how you manage the presentation of content in your course. Behaviorist strategies can be used to teach facts, cognitivist strategies can be used for principles and processes, and constructivist strategies can be used for higher-level thinking that promotes personal meaning and contextual learning. Connectivism suggests that knowledge resides in the network rather than in individuals. For us, using the Internet and Web-based tools is about building collaborations within and outside the confines of any classroom. The virtual classroom extends to wherever information might be found, shared, and discussed. Teaching and learning online is about making connections to improve the thinking and ideas of the class community.

How Will You Deliver Content?
How will your learners acquire their knowledge of the content? Palloff and Pratt (2013) suggest

- electronic textbooks with interactive activities,
- assignments that develop Web research skills,
- collaborative work that helps students learn from one another, and
- assignments that encourage learners to gain expertise in one content area and share it with their colleagues.

You may not have to develop your content from scratch. MERLOT (Multimedia Educational Resource for Learning and Online Teaching; www .merlot.org) offers links to free and open-source online learning materials.

Another source of content is your textbook publisher. Publishers often supplement textbooks with online materials. The emerging movement of open educational resources provides a wealth of content developed by subject matter experts worldwide. The Internet allows creating and sharing dynamic spaces where new ideas can evolve and merge with existing thoughts. Why invest time in repeating content that is readily available? The learner's task in an online collaborative classroom is to share and take what is known one step further.

Technology's Influence

A successful class is more than just the sum of its parts. A discussion, the content, activities, and the evaluation individually may mean little in terms of a worthwhile learning experience. Garrison (2011) defines a *worthwhile learning experience* as the product of actively engaged learners deeply reflecting on content together in an inquiry to achieve shared understanding about an issue or concern relevant to their lives. Combined, those experiences may assist students in developing a deeper understanding of a topic. Technology adds an additional layer to this scenario.

Considering the change from a physical classroom to an electronic classroom, you may want to reevaluate how you get across a particular topic. What may have worked well as an item on a PowerPoint slide now needs deeper explanation. Content presented in a face-to-face discussion may not work in a chat room; it may be better suited to a discussion board. Although text alone may have been suitable before, students may need further explanation with a video example and a discussion follow-up.

The Course Plan as a Way to Structure Content

Although we focus on the idea that an online course should not result in cognitive differences in perceived learning, that does not mean that methods of teaching the material remain the same. It is not a one-to-one conversion. Unfortunately, there isn't a heuristic that reveals exactly how your specific content is going to change. It is a function of teaching style, technology, specific content, time invested in course development, and the experience of teaching online. The Internet is a multimedia carrier of information. Content can be displayed in video, audio, print, or any combination of formats.

When working through the course plan, it is sometimes difficult not to frame activities through specific technologies. If you think you want a chat room discussion, or audio clips, ask yourself why. How does using a specific technology help you achieve your learning goals for the class? Our recommendation is to keep the technologies in mind and to be aware of the possibilities but use those technologies only where appropriate. For example, chat doesn't work for everything, and chat in big classes can become overwhelming.

Writing a course plan prior to the development of a full-course syllabus can link time (weeks for specific content modules) with the course and module learning objectives, with materials, and with activities. In a knowledge-building environment, learners will require a base level of knowledge before going on to critique the existing knowledge base and begin to generate original thoughts.

Course materials and assessments should show students how they are progressing from being dependent on the authoritative texts to becoming critical of the texts to becoming secure in their abilities to work together as a group and begin to build on one another's understandings. Aside from focusing on content, the course plan (see Table 3.2) will also need to build skills in being a member of a collaborative working group. For instructors in a knowledge-building course, the focus is more on helping learners identify resources rather than providing direct links to content.

TABLE 3.2
Suggested Course Plan

Date and Course Goal	Course Objectives	Readings, Activities and Assignments, Assessments
Week 1: Prepare to teach online.	Assess readiness to teach in an online or blended environment. Describe ways to manage time and establish relationships.	1.1. Read textbook Introduction, Chapters 1–3. 1.2. Watch video presentation. 1.3. Complete technical and attitudinal assessments. 1.4. Write a course communication plan.
Week 2: Select appropriate tools.	Describe when to use threaded discussions. Distinguish between when to use file sharing or discussion boards. Demonstrate how to use news items. Demonstrate how to use communication tools.	2.1. Read textbook Chapter 4. 2.2. Watch video presentation. 2.3. Build learner interaction spaces in lab course. 2.4. Build a "Before You Begin" space. 2.5. Set up intro news item. 2.6. Discussion 2: Types of interactions

Course Calendar

It is also helpful to prepare a course calendar listing the due dates for various assignments. This will give online students a sense of how to allocate their time and prepare them for making the decision to stay in the course. The course calendar also helps you determine if the time allocations for various activities are realistic. We have learned that some discussions and some activities will take longer than one week per module. Because online students are engaging in multiple activities, having a schedule in advance helps learners make room in their busy lives for group activities. (See Table 3.3 for an example of a course calendar.)

The course plan and the course calendar begin to develop the rhythm and flow of the learning and illustrate how each week learners will move from dependency to interdependency. These materials are often included in a start-up section of an online course. This introductory module is usually available to students prior to the start of the course. (We more fully explain the function of the "Start Here" or "Before You Begin" module in Chapter 6.)

TABLE 3.3
Sample Course Calendar

Saturday/ Sunday	Monday	Tuesday	Wednesday	Thursday	Friday
	Course starts Discussion: Topic 1 Assignment 1: Learner profile Quiz: Quiz 1		Discussion: Topic 1 initial post due		Discussion: End Topic 1 Quiz: Quiz 1 due
Assignment 1: Learner profile due	Discussion: Topic 2 Assignment 2: Weekly reflection		Discussion: Topic 2 initial post due		Discussion: End Topic 2
Assignment 2: Weekly reflection due	Discussion: Topic 3 Assignment 3: Weekly reflection		Discussion: Topic 3 initial post due		Discussion: End Topic 3

(Continues)

TABLE 3.3 (*Continued*)

Saturday/ Sunday	Monday	Tuesday	Wednesday	Thursday	Friday
Assign- ment 3: Weekly reflection due	Discussion: Topic 4 Assignment 4.1: Term project Assignment 4.2: Weekly reflection		Discussion: Topic 4 initial post due		Discussion: End Topic 4
Assign- ment 4.2: Weekly reflection due	Discussion: Topic 5 Assignment 5: Weekly reflection		Discussion: Topic 5 initial post due		Discussion: End Topic 5
Assign- ment 5: Weekly reflection due	Discussion: Topic 6 Assignment 6: Weekly reflection		Discussion: Topic 6 initial post due		Discussion: End Topic 6
Assign- ment 6: Weekly reflection due	Discussion: Topic 7 Assignment 7: Weekly reflection		Discussion: Topic 7 initial post due		Discussion: End Topic 7
Assign- ment 7: Weekly reflection due	Discussion: Topic 8 Assignment 8: Weekly reflection		Discussion: Topic 8 initial post due		Discussion: End Topic 8
Assignment 8: Weekly reflection due Assignment 4.1: Term project due					

A very important use of the course plan and the course calendar is to create activities and assignments that develop skills in content and skills in group learning processes. Your content is created in a safe environment that allows success and activities that build on skills previously acquired.

According to Boettcher and Conrad (2016), an online course has four stages, with each phase dedicated to more complex activities and assignments. In Stage 1, beginnings, the instructor has the main role of establishing the architecture for the course and providing opportunities for students to identify their interests and concerns, experiment with tools, communicate, and begin to form relationships. In our courses, we allocate at least one class and a precourse activity for the getting-to-know-you-and-each-other tasks, becoming familiar with the navigation, and stating interests in the subject matter.

Stage 2, early middle, establishes the rhythm of the class. We introduce content to the whole class and begin the process of whole-class discussions in the form of initial and response posts. Learners are acquiring foundational knowledge and locating resources. In this phase we move the students from whole class to smaller group discussions with final postings back to the whole class. This phase lasts about three weeks.

In Stage 3, late middle, teams are formed to investigate issues of common concern. As instructors, we note the interests and form initial teams that are fluid for the next week as learners sort out their interests and connect with others. Content is still being acquired; however, the content is now generated from the discussion boards. We are moving to the periphery and learners are moving toward the center. We are also moving from individual posts to cooperative activities.

In Stage 4, closing weeks, learners are immersed in the new content emerging from their study in the form of collaborative groups. When and how these phases occur is part of the course plan and course structure. Boettcher and Conrad (2016) suggest thinking in terms of what the learner is doing; the particular role of the instructor; the content knowledge acquired, synthesized, and generated; and the environment (i.e., meeting spaces and tools).

Fifth Concern: How Does My Teaching Persona Change?

The fifth concern is the change in teaching persona. Your teaching persona is developed from the instructional and philosophical stances guiding your instruction, your interactional style, and your goals for learners. Personas also are context dependent, meaning the profiles are rooted in the nature of your subject matter and your experiences in the classroom, which influence how you shape a particular instructional environment. Teaching styles do change in an inquiry-based online teaching-learning environment. In an online environment, your students come to know you through the design of your course, your engagement in and enthusiasm for the subject matter, your instructional policies, assignments, and the support and resources offered individually and collectively. Who you are as an instructor can change from being a content presenter and evaluator to an active partner in shaping the learning of the class members through your own dialogue with them in the search for shared understanding. We do not mean to discount the value of individual learning in terms of knowledge acquisition or grappling with difficult content. However, aside from convenience, the strength of the Internet is in the networks we build and in the power of discovery from seeing the thoughts emerge from others and from being able to assemble the best thinking from the collective to address an important topic.

In the online environment, the instructor as the primary source of content morphs into the instructor as curator, organizing and assembling resources, instructional notes, and readings. The instructor becomes a facilitator helping learners to form questions, challenge their statements, and push the thinking to higher critical levels of thought.

Teaching style can influence learning by synchronizing the student's attributes as a learner with the instructor's teaching style (Felder & Brent, 2005). Understanding the limits and possibilities of your teaching style may be helpful as you make the transition to the facilitative online learning environment. Grasha (1994, 1996) identified five teaching styles that represented typical orientations and strategies college faculty use to promote learning: expert, formal authority, personal model, facilitator, and delegator. Given different subject matter, course goals, and beliefs about how knowledge is created, transmitted, and applied, we expect online instructors to have varying proportions of each style.

According to Grasha (1994, 1996), the styles converge into four clusters that characterize how instructors design and facilitate courses.

The expert and formal authority cluster is teacher centered and works best with students who are unfamiliar with the content. Because the instructor controls how the content is presented, the flow of information, and how class time is spent, different learning styles are generally not considered.

The personal model, expert and formal authority cluster is centered around the instructor as role model and coach guiding students to develop and apply skills and knowledge. Instructors are sensitive to different learning styles and encourage the development of collaborative skills.

The facilitator, personal model, and expert cluster emphasizes collaborative and student-centered learning processes. Students need to be willing to take initiative and instructors are less interested in controlling specific details of the content students acquire. Generally, instructors in this cluster are more concerned with developing broader skills, such as critical and creative thinking skills.

The delegator, facilitator, and expert cluster emphasizes independent learning activities. Instructors give up direct control over how learners engage in various activities and produce learning outcomes. The instructor acts as a resource person and consultant for learners who take initiative and accept responsibility for their own learning.

Awareness of Learning Styles

Awareness of different learning styles may assist you to take a balanced approach to facilitating online learning activities, which is necessary to accommodate the diverse needs of students as you link learning goals and facilitation methods to appropriate learning theories. Riechmann and Grasha (1974) have identified six learning styles: independent, avoidant, collaborative, dependent, competitive, and participant.

It is important to match your teaching style to the expectations of the learners. What would you do if your style is not compatible with that of your learners? For example, you are a text-based, formal authority, and your learners are more visual and collaborative. How would you reconcile your differences?

We do note that the facilitator style is the most predominant in an inquiry-based online course. Of course, this does not mean that the expert style is devalued. As an instructor, your knowledge is shared rather than stated in an authoritative manner. Examining your profile is an interesting exercise and may reflect your inner thoughts about teaching and learning.

Insights From a New Online Instructor

I think that the aspect that is lacking in my online instruction that definitely needs improvement for the benefit of my students' learning needs and styles is the implementation and incorporation of collaborative and cooperative learning. This presence can be achieved fairly easily by giving my students a platform for discussion and providing a safe online environment where they can socially engage to discuss content from the course.

We recommend that instructors be flexible in their approach to instruction, seek out information about learning styles, and incorporate various activities that address different ways students learn.

The five big concerns (i.e., the online instructional platform, shifting time, flexible learning spaces, content presentation, and flexible teaching styles) begin to change the way instructors and learners develop relationships, communicate, and learn from each other. A common thread connecting the five concerns is flexibility. Online spaces change as technology changes, as learners and instructors become more comfortable developing a presence and an identity through a machine interface. We become electronically and yet humanly connected.

Points to Remember

- Tour your online instructional platform to see the spaces available for posting content and encouraging interaction among learners.
- Think of class time in terms of 24-hour days rather than a few hours per week.
- Use content pages for knowledge acquisition and discussion boards for knowledge generation.
- Write a course plan to link time with the course and module learning objectives and with materials, activities, and assessments.
- Prepare a course calendar listing the due dates for assignments.

For Reflection

1. Complete the Attitude Toward Online Teaching Questionnaire in Appendix B.
2. Which statements do you most strongly disagree with? What are your assumptions related to those statements? To what extent are you open to reading information that may contradict your beliefs?

4

THINKING AND ACTING LIKE AN ONLINE INSTRUCTOR

My greatest personal challenge with online instruction, I feel, has been and will continue to be finding and implementing strategies that will keep my students engaged and interested in our online courses and in our program.

—Kim, beginning online teacher

I believe my biggest challenge in teaching an online course will be the difficulty of text being the primary source of communication. I am a "people person." I fear that I will not be able to build the important student/teacher relationships needed to effectively instruct a course without face-to-face contact. Perhaps I will find ways to incorporate more audio/visual technology in my virtual classroom as a way to combat these fears. Tools such as video chatting would make me feel less isolated and help bridge the gap between myself and the students.

—Craig, beginning online teacher

From our work with many beginning online instructors, we find that many doubt their ability to convey a sense of themselves as the instructor, to know their learners if they cannot see them or hear their voices, to give immediate feedback, and to see the reactions of the learners to the material they present.

Many instructors are overwhelmed with the amount of activity that goes on in discussion boards as well as the needs of students to hear from the instructor. An online course management plan is needed to help you navigate, communicate, read, and respond to the thoughts of the learners in your class. In doing so, you will develop a supportive relationship with your learners. In this chapter we discuss five ways to help you establish yourself as an online instructor. After completing this chapter, you will be able to do the following:

- Determine a time of day to be online
- Develop a communication plan that states how and when you will converse with your learners
- Compose a time management plan to balance online teaching with other aspects of your life
- Develop a sense of comfort with the unpredictability of student learning and a sense of trust that students will learn from each other and the course materials
- Establish an online persona through your words and actions

Be Present

Perhaps the most important action for an online instructor is to be present online. When we hear stories of why online learning is not successful for many students, it is because of a lack of instructor presence. One struggling student noted that her course "involved rote memorization and drill—not the more challenging tasks of reading complex texts and making intelligent statements about those texts." Remember, online teaching is not meant to be an electronic correspondence course, given the expectations of students and the tools learners use every day to engage with content. Learners need structure in the design of the course and guidance from the instructor throughout the course. An online course is not completed when the content, assignments, and assessment tools are posted. That is just the beginning of the experience.

Set aside a time of day to respond to messages just as if you were meeting at an on-campus class. Rather than being in a classroom once or twice a week, being online requires your presence throughout the week. The idea is for you to be present in the learning space. As a guideline, we recommend being present at least three times per week at a minimum (if a module lasts one week) in the discussion room sharing ideas, suggesting resources, and posing questions to raise the level of cognitive thought. Your institution might also establish minimum guidelines for posting in your online classroom. Your students will know that you are there, reading and responding to their postings and assignments. Your students and administrators of your institution expect for you to be present at certain times throughout the week. You might vary the times during the week to see when and who is posting at different times. You might even find that you see messages popping up on your screen. Some instructors hold a weekly synchronous session to address questions and concerns, review content, and provide guidance on upcoming assignments and activities.

We have found that students will post almost every hour throughout a 24-hour period. In an online learning environment, participants in your course are posting messages, asking questions, and e-mailing you every day all day. It is instructive to check the time stamps on postings because you will see the working patterns that your learners are bringing to your course. A product of anytime messaging is that the learners expect for you too to be always available and ready to respond to their questions. The online world has made instant response an expectation. Having clear and consistent guidelines for how and when you respond can reduce learner anxiety about knowing that help is available.

Insights From a New Online Instructor

While it's wonderful that I can receive messages and respond to students on my phone, sometimes the constant stream of communication can leave me less focused on the tasks of the class. Being accessible, receiving communication from students, and managing an online class at all times of the day, and in different places, leaves me feeling scattered and disorganized. One of the ways I have tried to adjust to this is to block out times in my day when I will respond to students and take care of class business. When non-urgent matters present themselves outside of those blocks of time, I save them until my next "appointment" with the class. This allows me to be present for students, while still maintaining a sense of organization and focus.

Time Management Plan

We recommend developing a time management plan as you would in a physical classroom. On what days and at what times will you respond to e-mails, check and comment in the discussion boards, post grades, write a weekly summary, and open and close the modules?

A new online instructor told us that separating online teaching time from other obligations is a critical issue. Let your students know when you will be available for meetings via e-mails, phone, or video conferencing links. We usually tell students that we will respond to e-mails within 24 hours. An online learner offered guidance to "set clear expectations with learners at the beginning of the course. . . . As long as everyone is on the same page at the start, it should go smoothly" (J. Wells, personal communication, September 27, 2015).

Stavredes (2011) suggests writing a weekly time management plan corresponding to the start and end days for your class. She estimates that with 20 learners in a dialogue-based course, you should expect to invest 10 to 15 hours, depending on the level and structure of the course.

Using a weekly schedule, estimate the time you take to accomplish course management and instructional tasks. Record the actual time it takes. It is important to map out the days that you will accomplish instructional tasks. For example, we post a weekly summary on the course home page every Monday at 10:00 a.m. We check the discussion board every other day for 30 to 45 minutes in the morning and again in the afternoon or early evening. The time may vary depending on the number of daily posts and comments. This way we can catch the daytime and evening posts.

Having a time management plan lets you establish your own rhythm for the class. Establish parameters for being online so that your online teaching does not take over your other responsibilities. We have found that being present in the virtual classroom on a consistent basis will create a sense of being there for your students.

In our experience, learners want to know that you are there, reading and commenting on posts, keeping the discussion flowing, asking questions, suggesting resources that can deepen the learning, and, at the very least, monitoring the interactions among the students; between the students and the content; and with you, the instructor.

Insights From a New Online Instructor

It is not easy to balance everything. I am currently teaching online at three schools, and it is much more challenging and time consuming to teach classes online. I am present in my classes about five out of seven days a week, and I look at the course modules so that I do not forget anything. I also take my laptop with me wherever I go.

Predictable Presence

Our practice is to establish a predictable presence. We recommend being present at least three times per week (if a module lasts one week) at a minimum in the discussion room sharing ideas, suggesting resources, and posing questions to raise the level of cognitive thought. Just a few minutes every day shows the learners that you are involved in the course as a facilitator, subject matter expert, coach, and colearner.

In the beginning of the course, more time might be needed to model appropriate ways of interacting online. Online learning for many learners is not meant to be an independent study experience. The amount of guidance needed from the instructor will vary as the course intensifies and as the learners become more interdependent. Before teaching online, develop your plan, post your plan, and work your plan.

Insights From a New Online Instructor

In order to encourage healthy, achievable expectations on the part of students, an instructor can provide explicit feedback and directions, thus cutting down on the number of questions students must ask about any given assignment. Students can be assured of a response within 24 hours and can be instructed in the syllabus to wait 24 hours before sending a follow-up e-mail. An instructor can give students a sleep schedule along with the syllabus, for example: "I will be asleep from 10:00 p.m. to 6:00 a.m. EST every single night, and cannot answer e-mails during this time." That said, an online instructor absolutely must commit to checking e-mails and messages and logging in to the e-learning system at least once a day. There is simply no getting around this fact.

Be Communicative

A communication plan states how and when you will converse with your learners and the type of tools you will use (Stavredes, 2011). For example, you might consider when it is appropriate to use e-mail to communicate with your learners. E-mail pushes messages to the students, whereas messages posted on the Web require students to log in to the course site. How might you use announcements (sometimes labeled as news)? Announcements can be used to alert students of upcoming activities, reminders about assignments, and summaries of the class's accomplishments. Texting reminders about due dates or ideas to consider keeps students engaged and involved in the course. A short text message about an exciting reading or a resource can help students master the material.

Will you use the discussion board for feedback? We tell learners to post concerns that might be of interest to the entire class on the discussion board and to send an e-mail when it is a private concern.

Another consideration is determining when you will respond to e-mails or questions about the course. In an age of instant communication, people expect instant responses. In an online environment, learners cannot ask you questions after class. An unanswered e-mail can cause great anxiety. Planning to respond to e-mails within 24 to 48 hours is reasonable. The general rule might be the sooner the better and not let e-mails age; an e-mail is not a fine wine. The syllabus could include your reply-and-response cycle. Learners tell us that they desire this level of predictability.

Insights From a New Online Instructor

My overall concern is being able to truly connect with students and harvest collaborative and open communication online. I know it can be done, but I also know that it is a challenge because everyone communicates differently. For a lot of students (young and old), they have struggles transitioning from the traditional classroom and course communication to something that is 100% virtual. I think my strategy will be to use message boarding to establish relations, trust, and a sense of community; but then to offer virtual office hours via video conferencing and make it a requirement to have at least one or two (depending on class size) virtual video conferences between the instructor and student during the course. I try to be personable in my teaching and I want to ensure that that connection and feeling resonates online.

Be Balanced

As an instructor, you have academic office hours and a life outside the university, including a family, other work and community commitments, and nonacademic interests and activities. For some instructors, having an online presence is also combined with physical classroom responsibilities, as in a blended or flexible course model.

Given our inclination to be available to our students as well as the curiosity concerning what is going on online, we have found that online courses can take all your available time or at least make you feel guilty if you are not online. Setting boundaries for your own personal and academic life is essential to survive in an online world.

A new online instructor has told us about online creep, the phenomenon you experience when your online work begins to take over your weekends and begins to interfere with your family life. David Stein, this book's coauthor, admits to spending many evenings having a casual conversation with friends, colleagues, and even family members while surreptitiously answering e-mails, reading discussion threads, responding on the discussion board, or thinking about the weekly course update. In an electronic course, class time is always on.

Insights From a New Online Instructor

[As an adjunct,] organizing my time is clearly something that I struggle with because I have a difficult time balancing the different roles of my position sometimes. With an online class on top of my regularly assigned duties I simply don't have the option of not taking work home with me. I like the idea of having set virtual office hours and developing a plan of when specifically to work on my course. I'm hoping that will help me with time management concerns.

Be Comfortable

A prerequisite to thinking like an online teacher is developing a sense of comfort with the unpredictability of student learning and trusting that students will learn from each other and from the materials presented in the course.

Trust means you believe that learners will show up in their learning spaces at the times developed by the group, they will read the resources and come prepared to increase their understanding, and they will assist in the learning of the entire class. Trust means one is ready to stand back but not abdicate the overall teaching responsibility and yet realize that teaching presence means that everyone contributes to advancing the development of the group and dealing with the issues agreed to in the syllabus and in the course expectations.

Feeling comfortable with uncertainty is being okay with not knowing exactly what the learners are learning at a given time. It means giving up control of the spaces and letting the learners develop their content based on very general directions or topics provided by you. Uncertainty means stepping back and letting the learners take ownership, set the pathway, and build their understanding. You are there to offer support, address questions, and gingerly step in when the group is simply unable to move forward. In inquiry-based classes, the participants are on the stage, and we are there to provide the lines of the script only when it is certain that the show cannot go on.

When learners take control of the flow of the course and begin to generate their own learning, we have to be comfortable that the knowledge produced is meaningful to that group's improvement rather than relying on our own preconceived notions of what the students should produce. If the product meets the criteria for good scholarship in our fields, then the learners have met the overall course goals and have demonstrated mastery in ways that are connected to their experiences and to their interactions.

If you as an instructor are ready to reduce your control over every aspect of the educational space, and if you are ready to invite and promote learner participation in the design and implementation of the activities and artifacts produced, then you are ready to step inside an online course that promotes student ownership of the learning experience and moves the students to increased levels of confidence in their ability to master the course content.

Establish an Online Persona

In an online teaching and learning environment, students will know you mostly by your words, the text messages you create to inform, instruct, and improve the academic performance. Consider your writing style and evaluate the tone of the messages. How do you think the students are hearing your voice? Is the content of your messages clear? In an online world, particularly in asynchronous class designs, the learner does not have an opportunity to ask questions immediately about the assignments, due dates, or course procedures. Is the tone of your message warm and encouraging? Learners may feel anxious about being in an environment without immediate access to the instructor and may need support and encouragement to feel connected to you. Does the tone of your messages convey confidence in your knowledge of the topic without overwhelming the students?

Insights From a New Online Instructor

The smiley face serves an incredibly vital purpose. It shows my tone is light and humorous. Imagine adding that smiley to the end of a criticism or an admonition, and you understand its utility. In real life, we soften our corrections with a sympathetic smile or a calm voice. We let people know we are indulging in sarcasm with our laughter. Smilies of various types and shapes allow us to do exactly the same thing on the Internet, thereby lowering the odds of conflict with our students. You may even try the occasional encouraging digital image. And if you find your students still can't always understand your intentions, there is always the option of explicit feedback.

In an online teaching environment, the instructor becomes a curator for learning. Fifty-minute lectures or long pages of text will not keep learners involved in the learning process. We think of the online instructor as locating and assembling materials for learning, which includes scanning the Web for the high-quality resources needed for a particular learning objective and explaining how to use the resources and what to gain from them. Resources might include print materials, audio and video materials, and links to other websites as well as explanatory and summative statements about the content needed to meet academic performance standards. The online persona changes from the sole source of content to one who helps learners work with content.

To further convey your persona, you might want to produce a short video clip introducing yourself and your philosophy of instruction. You can create a short video using a webcam and a screen capture program such as Tegrity (mheducation.com/highered/platforms/tegrity.html) or Screencast-O-Matic (screencast-o-matic.com). You can also produce an audio message in PowerPoint with an image of yourself. Live Web conferencing can be used at the beginning, middle, and end of your course to further develop your persona and invite students to interact with you and with each other. One caveat: You may have to plan multiple sessions to accommodate different time schedules. Learners tell us that seeing us and hearing our voices early in the course cycle produces a sense of connection and affirms that there really is an instructor out there.

Points to Remember

- Establish and implement a time management plan.
- Develop a communication plan that states how and when you will converse with your learners.
- Balance online teaching with other aspects of your life.
- Develop a sense of comfort with the unpredictability of student learning; trust that students will learn from each other and the course materials.
- Establish an online persona via your words and actions.

For Reflection

1. Refer to the Communication Plan Template in Appendix C and the Communication Plan Checklist in Appendix D.
   a. Develop a communication plan that states how and when you will converse with your learners.
2. Refer to the Time Management Plan Checklist in Appendix E.
   a. Develop a time management plan for your course.

SECOND CHALLENGE

BUILDING ONLINE SPACES FOR LEARNING

BUILDING SPACES AND PLACES FOR LEARNING

Online learning is more than just posting materials and videos and asking a few questions. It requires a lot of thought and organization up front so that your learners get the most out of their experience. You can offer various learning activities, such as group work, message boards, blogs, and chats to engage with students. By varying instructional delivery and activities, you can create active, personal, and dynamic learning opportunities for students.

—Li, learner in an online class

Instructors who have never taught online (or taken a class online) may be unsure of how to reach students in an online setting or even how to set up (construct) an online class.

—Susan, beginning online teacher

We have often been asked by our online learners and especially other faculty about where the teaching and learning happens. Given an emphasis on learning as knowledge acquisition, it is easy for most instructors to visualize instruction happening in the classroom where information is exchanged, processed, and measured in a regularly scheduled time and place. Learning is assessed on the basis of individual demonstrations of academic products (tests, papers, and artifacts that represent individual effort). Less certain is learning that involves participation in shared group activities. In this chapter we discuss the instructor's role in building the spaces and places for learners to interact with content, the instructor, other learners, and their own thoughts. After completing this chapter, you will be able to do the following:

- Describe the function of learning spaces that promote interaction
- Identify various private and public spaces for learners and the role they play in learning
- Define *community space*

- Explain the role of spaces for nonacademic talk
- Assess the utility of various technology tools for your course

Integrated Spaces

Where does the learning happen online? What do we see and hear in the electronic spaces? How do we make visible the public thoughts and the voices of our learners when they cannot be heard in the classroom or when we cannot observe interactions directly to see that learning is or is not happening? How do we construct spaces for sharing and interaction in a manner that facilitates learning?

In the electronic classroom, learning happens online and offline throughout the week. Learners can return to discussion boards and other spaces set up for collaborative activities. The spaces we create for interaction embody the virtual presence of our learners. In the spaces we create, our learners can use electronic tools to produce video, audio, or print messages.

For us, the online classroom is an integration of spaces for content presentation, content sharing, resources used to expand on content, spaces to reflect on one's own private thoughts about content, and spaces to engage in dialogue with others and the instructor about class and other related matters. Spaces can be created for individual and small-group and whole-class learning, depending on the degree of interaction designed into your classes.

In our courses, we try to make visible learners' thoughts and comments, which lead to new knowledge. The spaces lead to what Hakkarainen (2004) has called *epistemic agency*, and we agree with the notion that it is the instructor's responsibility to build the spaces but not tightly control all the content that occupies these spaces. Some spaces belong to the students as they become more aware of their own thoughts and their own agency in creating novel ideas arising from their study of content.

Spaces are used for learners to realize their own views on the content, individually and collectively; to work with others to develop an understanding using their own intellectual resources; and to reflect on the learning that is arising from integrating text, class conversations, instructor comments, and other resources available in cyberspace.

Insights From a New Online Instructor

The teaching happens through the lessons and activities, but the learning happens in the offline environment where the participants can reflect, develop their responses, gather any additional inputs, review their responses, and return online to contribute when they are ready. The discussion space is where much of the engagement takes place through the use of required postings and responses. As the participants re-engage, their learning is enhanced by viewing the responses from their peers and incorporating that into their own understanding.

Interaction: A Key Component

Interaction is a core component of online teaching and is necessary to sustain learner interest and commitment to participating at a distance. As an instructor, what are your assumptions about the kinds of interactions your learners need and expect? As a learner, what kinds of interactions support your learning? We conceptualize the learning space as being composed of five interactions. The three most common types of interaction discussed in the distance education literature are learner-content, learner-instructor, and learner-learner. A fourth type, instructor-and-learner-interface interaction, acknowledges the interaction that occurs when instructors and learners use intervening technologies to design and participate in online courses. In our courses, we add spaces for a fifth type of interaction: learner reflection or learner-to-self interaction. This is a space for self-dialogue where learners can challenge their own notions based on content presented as well as the ideas and thoughts arising from class discussions. Our course design features spaces that encourage and support each type of interaction.

Learner-Content Interaction

Learner-content interaction is characterized by learner acquisition of subject matter for the primary purpose of gaining information. Guided individual or self-paced activities such as readings, Web-searching activities, and watching videos emphasize learner-content interaction. Learner-content interaction is the focus of many educational activities because we are used to thinking that content is the most important part of an educational event or because we have organizational constraints that limit the time instructors can spend with learners. One way to take advantage of an online environment when focusing on learner-content interaction is to use the visual, auditory, and kinesthetic (VAK) modalities model (Barbe, Swassing, & Milone, 1979). VAK suggests that each learning event should include visual, auditory, and kinesthetic approaches to presenting content. In the VAK framework, the senses describe the way students might acquire information. When designing a class activity, for example, make the three senses evident while conducting the activity. Content presentations might include text,

TABLE 5.1
Tools for Visual, Auditory, and Kinesthetic Learning

Visual	Auditory	Kinesthetic
• Screencasts: www.screencast-o-matic.com • Short videos: animoto.com • PowerPoint with narration: www.gcflearnfree.org/powerpoint2010/24.2 • Text-based discussions: www.lefora.com	• Podcasts, audio blogs: www.wikihow.com/Start-Your-Own-Podcast • Voki videos: voki.com	• Tools that help learners move objects around the screen; for example, matching and sorting activities, crossword puzzles: www.readwritethink.org • Cartoon development: www.pixton.com

video, and audio clips as well as graphics and quizzes that provide feedback on responses. Consider using media such as YouTube videos for instructional purposes, and require students to use the Internet to obtain content resources. Table 5.1 offers suggestions on tools you can use to appeal to your learners' different senses.

Learner-Instructor Interaction

Learner-instructor interactions include opportunities for participants to address or hear the voice (or text) of the instructor in support of the learning process. Learner-instructor interactions can be fostered through e-mail comments, an "Ask the Instructor" space, virtual office hours, and assessments. Learner-instructor interactions are also supported in discussion boards, announcements, and module summaries.

The online learning environment we create is conversational and dialogic; it is conversational in that we share our thoughts and concerns about everyday events related to the course as well as our own struggles in teaching online. (Sometimes we do not follow our time management plan or feedback cycle as life events intervene and we miss a deadline.) We model how we cope with the rhythms of online instruction, and we make adjustments when the rhythms are disrupted. For example, David Stein had a medical issue that affected the timeliness of feedback and informed the learners in the following message:

> Dear Learners, I was playing with my grandson, and now I may have a broken finger. Given that typing is a critical component for my interactions with you, I may be delayed in responding to your message and in posting content. I will try working with a voice recorder. Please forgive any delays in posting and responding to your messages.

We encourage our learners to share their stories and, in doing so, build cohesiveness as a component of social presence. Modeling sharing behaviors can contribute to building a safe space for learners to share their travails in living and learning in an online environment. Our goal is to find ways to accommodate the difficulties that might get in the way of instruction. We can only do this if learners feel comfortable sharing with us the circumstances that hinder their participation. When imagining how learner-instructor interactions can be facilitated, consider how familiar participants are with using various communication tools and how to interpret textual cues that substitute for visual cues that might be found in a face-to-face classroom.

Learner-Learner Interaction

Learner-to-learner interactions describe the ways learners share information without the presence of an instructor, engage in dialogue, and develop a shared understanding of the issues. Learner-learner interactions are the primary means participants use to begin to take ownership of the course and become knowledge creators. As such, learner-learner interactions are developed through collaborative spaces, such as wikis, social media sites, and discussion boards. Smyth (2011) suggests that learner-to-learner interactions can be fostered by designing activities promoting decision-making, problem-solving, case studies, or other activities in which multiple responses are possible in demonstrating acquisition and application of knowledge gained from learner-content interactions as well as knowledge created by frequent communications among the participants.

Learner-to-learner spaces can be cooperative or collaborative. It is instructive to briefly review the differences between *cooperative classrooms* and *collaborative classrooms* because the terms are sometimes used interchangeably and are not well established in instructional practice. The primary differences are in the control of the classroom, the way students work, and the type of products produced.

Cooperative learning. In a cooperative online classroom, information is shared among learners in a discussion board, for example, and tasks are divided up for individuals to complete. The separate pieces are assembled to address a situation or problem created by the instructor. The group creates a response that meets the criteria established by the instructor for an acceptable solution. Group members work independently and come together to knit a response from the separate and now connected thinking of the group. In a cooperative learning situation, the whole equals the sum of the parts. The whole is a shared understanding based on knowledge that comes from authorities located by the learners and monitored by the instructor (Brunk-Chavez & Miller, 2007).

Collaborative learning. In a collaborative classroom, learners work together and negotiate new meanings arising from the separate thoughts of the group. The outcome is a collective thought that goes beyond any of the separate parts. Text material is used to generate content that had not previously existed in the mind of any single learner. Members are interdependent, realizing that the product is greater than the sum of the individual and the group thought. Reliance for innovation is on the members of the group rather than on established texts or the instructor as an authority. The solution is novel, resulting in constructed knowledge. With this approach, it is difficult to separate any one learner's contribution from the product. In collaborative networked environments, each learner's thought becomes the input for a new thought by other members of the group (Schellens & Valcke, 2006).

In a collaborative environment, more responsibility is placed on the team to manage itself and to develop its processes for producing the product. However, the instructor is involved in modeling, guiding, and evaluating the processes of team development and content production. Palloff and Pratt (2011) recommend that the instructor stay present but not control the content-generating environment. The instructor can still guide, coach, and help the members through the stages of group development and conflict. In collaborative learning, the whole is greater than the sum of its parts.

Collaborative and cooperative assessment. In collaborative as well as cooperative learning environments, the instructor has the obligation to assess the quality of the product as well as the process and the participation of group members. Although this can be shared, the instructor has responsibility for the final assessment.

Interaction equivalency. Although we recommend having strong learner-to-learner interactions, we recognize that it is not always possible to build a course with equal degrees of interaction. You might find Anderson's (2003) notion of interaction equivalency useful as you design your online spaces. Anderson's interaction equivalency theorem states that deep, meaningful learning can occur as long as one of the three forms of interaction is very high. Anderson asserts, however, that high levels of more than one type of interaction likely result in a more satisfying educational experience. When designing a course, therefore, you can substitute one type of interaction for one of the others at the same level (hence the term *equivalency*) with little loss in educational effectiveness. Anderson (2003) offers the following implications:

- Student-teacher interaction has the highest perceived value among students, but there is only so much of the teacher to go around. Therefore, student-content interaction replaces student-teacher interaction in many mass education systems. Anderson considers teacher videos and use of automated teacher agents as forms of student-content interaction.
- Student-student interaction is critical for collaborative and cooperative tasks. Student-student interaction is less critical for learning designs based on cognitive and behaviorist learning theories.
- Content is valuable only if it engages students and leads to knowledge construction.

Engagement theory. Another way to envision learner-learner interaction is through engagement. Engagement theory was designed to provide guidance for teaching in technologically enhanced environments (Kearsley & Schneiderman, 1998). Although this is an older theory, we have been using the concept of relate-create-donate to explain the process of learning together: relate to learning through collaboration, create by using a project-based approach, and donate to the broader learning community (Kearsley & Schneiderman, 1998). We maintain that e-learning environments are suited for learning together. If we simply want to learn individually, we are missing the power of the networked environment the Internet offers.

Insights From a New Online Instructor

In some cases, I don't think interaction is necessary or appropriate. I don't think you need it in cases where the objective is to learn basic, factual content, where there isn't a whole lot of room for debate or disagreement. For instance, if I were teaching a math class online, I wouldn't want to plan much student-student interaction at all. I can see why it might be tempting to have students collaborate in groups to solve tricky problems, but I'm not convinced it would be beneficial, since you want everyone to grapple with the problems and try to work them out using their own resources. At the end of the class, they have to be able to solve things on their own.

Learner-Self Interaction

Reflection is an interaction with oneself in which individual thought is blended with the thoughts of the community. At the end of each learning episode, the individual learner comes to a deep understanding of the new content generated by integrating initial thought with the emerging thoughts of the community through the process of self-talk, which is reflection on the established propositions and processes used to arrive at an individual and collective meaning. Critical reflection on assumptions and critical self-reflection on assumptions are elements of learner-self interaction (Kreber, 2011). During critical reflection on assumptions, we step back and objectively assess where our thoughts come from. We consider what is told to us. During critical self-reflection on assumptions, we focus on our own thoughts and how they influence our own actions. We examine why we act on what we were told and how we formed our own interpretations.

For adults, learning is a process of making new meanings from our experiences and prior interpretations. We create a new or revised interpretation to engage in action. The action is the change. For learning to happen, we must have a prior experience to interpret or make an association with the new incoming data. We must have an intention to learn or at least a feeling that something is happening, and we have to be aware. The meaning is specific to the context we are experiencing, and the ability to critically reflect on our assumptions is key to understanding the experience. For example, we use a simple reflective writing technique by asking the following questions:

- In what ways did the contributions of the community influence your thoughts on the issue?
- How do your thoughts about the issue differ (or not) from your original posting?
- How did the emerging thoughts challenge your assumptions and values underlying your original posting?
- What is your new or revised understanding of the issue?

The learner-to-self interaction brings closure to the learning episode.

Instructor-and-Learner-Interface Interactions

Instructor-and-learner-interface interactions describe how learners and instructors are both able to use and understand the limits and advantages of e-teaching tools and the online instructional platform. The tools shape how we design and participate in an online instructional session. A study of the relationship between interface interactions and a successful instructional session showed

TABLE 5.2
Tools for Individual, Group, and Collaborative Learning in Community

Individual	Group	Community
YouTube	Twitter	Google Drive
Google Search	PowerPoint	Google+ and Hangouts
EverNote	WordPress	WordPress
Dropbox	Facebook	Facebook

that the majority of students (64%) agreed that instructor comfort and use of appropriate tools were critical factors in their learning (Danesh, Bailey, & Whisenand, 2015). As instructors, we must also gauge the comfort and competence of our learners in using e-tools as well as how the tools help or hinder the expression of content and each learner's ability to engage and communicate with others. In selecting tools, consider availability (we use only free tools in our course or those available through the online instructional platform), concerns for privacy (i.e., whether students have to provide sensitive information to access the tools), and the time it takes to learn how to use the tool. We also consider the extent to which tools promote individual, group, or collaborative learning in community (see Table 5.2).

Teaching and Learning Spaces

Online spaces can foster independent and interdependent learning. Spaces can enable individuals to obtain separate knowing and then to go beyond their own understandings and consider the ideas of others that are made possible by the resources inherent in the group and in the larger Web-based community. Learning spaces also let us as instructors see higher levels of thinking evolve, including developing critical and reflective thought and the search and engagement strategies used to build more complex understandings of content.

How do we create a worthwhile learning experience? We can start by building spaces that promote the different types of interaction. Learning spaces can be built around the ideas of knowledge acquisition, knowledge creation, knowledge application, and knowledge sharing.

The First Space: Weekly Content

As online instructors, we create the weekly space for providing direction, content, and context for learning by giving learners the basic tools and rules for conducting the inquiry. We subdivide the weekly teaching and learning space into the following sections:

- The Overview tab contains a statement of the weekly goal and the module objectives. This information describes the intended learning outcomes.
- The Session Notes tab provides the content. The session notes are abbreviated thoughts about the topic and guide the students through the readings and difficult concepts. This tab is no longer than two pages and can be provided in print, audio, or video formats.
- The Readings and Resources tab provides links to required and supplementary content materials. In our courses, the materials we select carry the content to a greater degree than our session notes.
- The Activities and Assignments tab provides the weekly activities that will assist the students to demonstrate their ability to apply the content.
- The Assessment tab contains rubrics and other information about how the work produced by the students will be evaluated.

The instructor has the lead role in establishing the overall problem arising from the junction of academic inquiry and real-world situations. In our courses we establish an issue relevant to the environment where our students live and work. We provide text material to start the inquiry, usually placing it in an online instructional platform's content modules. We also encourage students to seek out additional resources using the Web, other practitioners, and other subject matter experts.

In an assignment space, we pose a problem that addresses real-world concerns arising from the content, including policy, economic, political, or social concerns. We are careful to frame the problem in an open-ended way to encourage inquiry rather than a search for the right answer. In fact, we instructors do not have an answer in mind. We provide guidance and ask learners to pose their own questions about the issue.

The Second Space: The Reflective Space

Learners are provided with a private space for recording their emerging ideas about the issue from the readings, their interpretation of the readings, and materials gathered from other electronic environments as well as their personal experiences. This is similar to a paper journal. In the electronic environment, it might appear as a blog or a closed discussion board space. (e.g., the Evernote application is a useful tool for constructing a personal understanding of an issue.)

In this space learners individually replay the dynamics of their interactions with the intent of becoming more effective as group members and knowledge creators. In this space learners can imagine what happened, why it happened, and how to improve performance. Learners also use this space to reflect on how raw data are transformed to knowledge. Aside from creating the new ideas, students learn about the process of how individual thoughts become published for the community to act on. The inquiry not only is about the issue but also includes learning how to make meaning, how to negotiate ideas, how ideas are tested and validated in the empirical world, and how original opinions are refined and presented to a community as an expansion of our understanding of the wisdom possessed by a community.

Recording private knowledge ensures that the learner has something to share before joining the communal space. Learners have the responsibility to come to the shared space with reasoned comments and questions. Learners can label their thoughts as ideas (i.e., mental images stimulated from the course and other materials), problem analysis (i.e., thoughts regarding the issue under discussion, its meaning and content, as well as questions to get at the issues), explanations, commentary on content, and resource notes (i.e., materials that may be helpful in the group discussions). These notes are then brought forward to the shared space.

The Third Space: Chat or Sharing Space

In this space, learners negotiate meaning and search for a deeper understanding of the issue. In the shared chat space, useful for small-group interactions, learners come together to blend private understanding with group meaning-making.

This is the space where the work of generating knowledge is accomplished. Instructors have a role in establishing initial guidelines for working in this space and assisting the learners to make appropriate uses of time and the expertise that has been developed within each student. In this collaborative space, learners share their accumulated knowledge and write their own texts. In our courses we provide initial guidance on how to structure the space and organize time.

The following is an example of the guidance we provide:

> While you are chatting, designate a member to search for relevant material on the Web that might assist with your discussion. Search for documents that would reinforce the points or expand the argument. In addition to interacting with each other and the assigned content, interact with resources beyond the material provided in the text or initially brought to the shared space—material and human. Observe how a comment from a colleague will trigger a new thought or generate new questions or ideas.

We also provide guidance on how to structure a group for collaborative work, as in the following:

> Conventional guidance suggests that a discussion group might have a moderator who is responsible for leading the discussion, a recorder who captures the ideas and who may post a summary of the group discussion, and participant roles to query, challenge, and advocate for certain positions.

However, we have noticed that the moderator or recorder usually feels responsible for taking the raw material—the chat transcripts—and creating a response reflecting the views of the group after the chat has concluded. Even when we have asked for the moderator or recorder to ask for feedback from the group regarding the accuracy of the response, the group members generally agree with the statements produced. We note that the artifact produced may not reflect the voices and ideas expressed by the group. We provide the following guidance for structuring the time and preparing for summaries of the ideas emerging from the group:

> Consider a 2-to-1 allocation based on a 60-minute chat, leaving at least 20 minutes to write your collective post. Write at least a 1- to 2-paragraph group draft response before concluding your chat. Your recorder will need to clean up the text, include relevant links, and send the draft to the group for review and comment prior to posting to the whole-class discussion board.

In the shared space, learners go through cycles of raising triggering comments; exploring ideas generated from resources, comments, and experience; integrating emerging thoughts to form new patterns; and finally achieving resolution in the form of a tentative statement. Visual resources as well as literature and websites can be posted by any group member for use by the group.

The Fourth Space: The Break Room
This space is used to post learner introductions to begin building a sense of community and connections among the learners (i.e., learner-to-learner interactions). "Ask the Instructor" is a place for communicating with the instructor about questions that would benefit the entire group or even the class (i.e., learner-to-instructor interaction).

An additional space called the "Coffee Table" (suggested by a former learner) is used for students to converse with each other and share resources in an area for nonacademic talk. We encourage learners to stop in, bring their coffee, and leave a note for their colleagues (learner-to-learner interaction).

The Fifth Space: The Community Space
The community space provided for learners is in the form of an asynchronous discussion board. Artifacts produced from the emergent ideas and innovative thinking of the inquiry group are posted on a public community space for comment and feedback on the quality of the artifact and its originality.

The knowledge generated through collaborative exchanges is now subject to testing in a public exchange among other classmates or experts in the subject matter under inquiry. Comments posted by others in the community are meant to help the learners explore, test, and refine ideas posted. Our guidance in this space is as follows:

> Respond to at least one group posting. The purpose of the response post is to challenge, clarify, expand, and illuminate the thinking of the group. Your comments should be informed by questions that might arise from reading the post. If you agree with the thinking, state why. If you challenge it, cite evidence for your view. Opinion should be supported with your experiences and with content related to the question we are examining.

Each group member should read the responses from other class members regarding the group's original post.

Reconvene your chat group, discuss the feedback received, review your original thinking, and repost your new and improved understanding of the issue.

The key point is that groups reconvene, consider the feedback, and repost their deeper understanding of the issue. The new post reflects new knowledge, which raises new questions for other groups to consider in later classes. This space is used for whole-class discussions or for posting and sharing assignments. Leinonen and Kligyte (2002) suggest that spaces create a database of knowledge processes as well as individual connections to resources, ideas, and thoughts. Through the creation of spaces, we can see the links connecting individual private thoughts to emerging new ideas. We see higher levels of thinking evolve, including developing critical and reflective thought and the search and engagement strategies used to build more complex understandings of content.

Points to Remember

- Build learning spaces to promote learner-content, learner-learner, and learner-instructor interaction.
- Create a weekly space for direction, content, and the context for learning.
- Create a private space for learners to record their emerging ideas; create a shared space for learners to negotiate meaning.
- Create a break room for introductions, questions for the instructor, and nonacademic talk.
- Create a community space on discussion boards for groups to post their thinking for comment and feedback.

For Reflection

1. Explore the tools in Appendix F: Technology Tools.
2. Assess the tools of interest to you in light of the following questions:
   a. Does the tool help clarify concepts?
   b. Does the tool provide a different perspective?
   c. Does the tool add to the course experience and learning objectives?
   d. Does my institution provide support for the tool?
   e. Is the tool accessible and easy to use?

THIRD CHALLENGE

PREPARING STUDENTS FOR ONLINE LEARNING

6

PREPARING YOUR STUDENTS FOR ONLINE LEARNING

For maximum success, students should fully participate in the exchange of information, sharing ideas and collaborating with others. Those elements are just as important as the curriculum, materials, and teaching methods used.

—June, learner in an online course

Online courses require students to be proactive learners. Students must dive into the content each week so that they reach their own meaningful learning outcomes as well as the learning objectives for the course.

—Michael, online teacher

L earners enroll in online courses for a variety of reasons, including convenience, flexibility, their need to take courses that might overlap in real time, and sometimes because they have an interest in the subject matter but are unable to attend a face-to-face class. Regardless of the reasons, students have concerns about how an online course operates, how contact with the instructor and other students will be developed and sustained, and what help will be available when the technology fails and questions about content arise. After completing this chapter, you will be able to do the following:

- Describe how to create a connection with each learner
- Compose a welcome message for your learners
- Assess ways in which you and your students can learn about one another
- Explore various opportunities to familiarize your learners with the course site
- Provide reassurance that learning online works

65

Community of Inquiry

Learners in any online course will want assurance that they are not alone, that there is an instructor who cares and is concerned about the learning, and that the materials will be easily found. Learners will want to know they will be able to connect with others. Learners also want to know that their thoughts and written work will be recognized and respected, and that the online environment will be a safe place to express their opinions and concerns. Overall, learners want to know how a worthwhile learning experience will be created in an online learning environment

The community of inquiry model reflects the current thinking on how to build and sustain a worthwhile learning experience for online learners. The model is based on collaborative learning and assumes that learning occurs through the interaction of three overlapping elements: social presence, teaching presence, and cognitive presence (Garrison, Anderson, & Archer, 2000).

According to Garrison and colleagues (2000), social presence is the ability of learners to project their personal characteristics to others through affective, interactive, and cohesive talk. Teaching presence involves course design, discourse facilitation, and direct instruction. Cognitive presence involves meaning-making through sustained communication that explores topics, integrates information, and results in a resolution of the issue under discussion. The combination of the three presences can result in a learning experience that promotes higher levels of thinking. Building social presence, connections, trust, and feelings of belonging to a learning group are the tasks an instructor creates in the opening weeks of an online course.

Take a few moments and reflect on your first experience in an online course. What thoughts did you have about the nature of the experience? How did you go about developing class relationships? What were your concerns about online learning? If you have not taken an online course, use the experience of the first day of any new learning endeavor.

As you have been preparing yourself to teach online and creating the spaces where learning can happen, the learners also need to be prepared to engage with you, the content, and each other. In the early phases of an online course, it is important to develop social presence. The main points to remember about social presence are the following:

- Social presence must support learning. It is a means to an end.
- Socializing for its own sake is not what we mean by social presence.
- Social presence consists of interpersonal, open, and cohesive communication.

Social Presence Supports Learning

Social presence is purposeful communication that supports inquiry and learning. In an academic context, Garrison (2011) says that social presence means "creating a climate that supports and encourages probing questions, skepticism, and the contribution of explanatory ideas" (p. 32). Social presence helps learners feel safe sharing their perspectives in an educational environment.

Socializing Is Not Social Presence

Online learners can feel isolated, especially if their primary interaction is with content. That's why we feel that in an inquiry-based course, where there are no right or wrong answers, it's important to establish relationships with others through learner-learner interaction and learner-instructor interaction. However, cultivating relationships for purely social purposes can undermine learning. When it's used appropriately, social presence can help advance a discussion when the participants indicate agreement or disagreement, greet one another, and share information about themselves.

Social Presence Is Interpersonal, Open, and Cohesive

Garrison (2011) illustrates what social presence looks like. Interpersonal communication involves emotions, personal disclosures, expressions of vulnerability, and use of humor and irony. Open communication continues a discussion thread rather than starting a new one, refers explicitly to others' messages, quotes from those messages, expresses appreciation or agreement, and asks questions of others. Cohesive communication refers to others by name, uses inclusive pronouns such as *we, us,* or *our* and serves a social function through greetings and closures.

Social Presence **Defined**

Given these three main points about *social presence*, Garrison (2011) defines the construct as "the ability of participants to identify with the group or course of study, communicate purposefully in a trusting environment, and develop personal and affective relationships progressively by way of projecting their individual personalities" (p. 34).

Rheingold (2000) presents a history of computer-mediated communications and the development of virtual communities. He makes an interesting comment about the idea of social presence and the importance of "idle talk" (p. xvii). The term *social presence* was not in his vocabulary at the time when his text was written in 1993 (and when most of us were not involved in electronic mailing lists, Internet conversations, etc.). He said that idle talk is context setting, which is how you establish an identity. How much you share and what you share helps others gain a sense of trust in you, come to learn about your interests, and gauge your willingness to share with the group rather than only take from the group.

Without a sense of trust and without a sense of the person, it is difficult to build a space where one can be free to share, express opinions, offer comments, or challenge prevailing ideas, in essence a community that values inquiry. Without the idea of social presence and without the time necessary to reacquaint and catch up, we may not be able to create a feeling of community, and we may not be ready to engage in intellectual activities, that is, cognitive presence.

Five Ways to Create Social Presence

You can begin creating social presence before your course starts by sending a welcome letter, posting your syllabus, and creating a "Start Here" or "Before You Begin" space. After your course is under way, foster social presence through introductions and regular news announcements.

Send Welcome and Expectations Messages

At least one week before the start of the class, send a welcome letter to your students. Include a brief biography to establish why you are qualified to teach the course. Your welcome message will set the tone for the work ahead and is one way to begin interacting with your students. The most important part of the message is your background. Because students will not be able to meet you directly, you can enhance the connections by sharing some information about yourself. This will also encourage others to disclose their interests. In your message use *we*, *us*, and *our* to communicate cohesiveness and a sense of community. The following are some of the elements to include in your welcome message:

- Contact information
- Link to the course
- Short description of the course
- How the course is designed
- Your philosophy of instruction
- Your background, interests, and hobbies

Your comments set the tone for the course. The welcome message is designed to create a supportive online environment for learning and begins to establish social and teaching presence. What are the typical concerns learners might have about an online course? How much time will it take? Where do they find materials? How will they be using the course features such as discussion boards, blogs, and journals?

Insights From a New Online Instructor

I believe much of what we call *relationship-building*, much of the boundary-negotiation process that undergirds online learning, starts with acknowledging that our online communication can be effective and real. . . . So much of the intention and inflection we attribute to face-to-face interactions is in fact fully possible with words alone. . . . We all, students and instructors alike, simply need to learn to pay more careful attention to word choice and brevity as well as verbosity.

Learners want to know the expertise of the instructor as well as how the instructor visualizes the goals of the course. This is an opportunity to create a first and lasting impression of yourself. The welcome message does not replace a syllabus nor should it contain the details of a syllabus. The welcome message begins establishing a supportive and intellectual climate. Appendix G contains an example of a welcome message developed by learners in our course about teaching adults online.

Welcome letters are used to provide an overview of the course conduct and operations. More detailed information about the course policies can be provided in a "Start Here" or "Before You Begin" section of the content module. We have recently asked students to send us an e-mail stating they have read the welcome letter and agree to follow the principles and practices described.

Following your welcome letter, send an expectations message to your students that gives learners insight into the goals for the course, the level of participation expected from them, and what they can expect from you. See Appendix G for a sample expectations message. Another aspect of establishing the learning environment is having learners state their expectations about the course, which can be done in an introduction posted in the course pages, providing them with a set of specific questions about themselves, or asking them to state their learning objectives or goals for the course. If you decide to have learners state their objectives or goals, be sure to follow up on it at the end of the course by asking them to reflect on how well their objectives or goals were achieved. The following are some of the elements to include in your expectations message:

- Responsibilities of learners and the instructor
- What learners can expect from you
- Expectations for frequency and content of posts
- What to do if there is a problem or concern

The expectations message establishes a common understanding of the expectations for the instructor and the learner. It also begins to involve the learners in the course materials.

Post Your Syllabus

Post your online course syllabus prior to the start of the first session and ask for feedback on the syllabus. Remember, in an online course students will not have an opportunity to directly ask you questions about the syllabus as in a face-to-face class. Include

- instructor contact information;
- course description of the overall intent of the course in a paragraph, which is used to build interest;
- overall course learning goals, which provide the broad outcomes for the course used to assess the degree to which the learner obtains the important points of the course;
- required texts and other course materials, including required and supplementary materials used to provide course content or activities;
- the course plan showing module learning objectives, content outline, assignments, and due dates, which shows the weekly activities (if the course is designed in a weekly format), the outcomes for each week, and the assignments to show the path to the outcomes;
- the grading plan showing points assigned to each graded assignment with the points needed to meet letter-grade levels, which can be in the form of a scale and provides information about how levels of performance will be assessed; and
- policy statements, including statements of academic honesty, support services, incomplete and late assignments, and special student needs, which show the policies that govern the class.

How is a syllabus for an online class different from a syllabus for a face-to-face class? In an online syllabus, also include

- a definition of what constitutes participation: logging in, posting messages in a discussion, collaborating in an online presentation, and so on, and an explanation of the credit or grade correlation to reinforce participation (a face-to-face syllabus might also have an in-class participation requirement);

- an explanation of how the class will work, specifically, how the student-instructor communication will occur and where to find the online syllabus;
- instructions to help students find the online classroom including perhaps a guide to navigation provided in an e-mail so students can locate the contents, readings, assignments, and how to use the tools for submitting assignments;
- due dates for initial posts and due dates for response posts, as in many online classes, the lesson may take place during a week rather than on a specific day, and time must be allocated for students to read materials, make a posting, and respond to classmates;
- rubrics for assessment that should be developed to clearly specify how assignments will be graded; and
- instructions for assignments that might be conducted in a face-to-face class but can be conducted online with clear instructions concerning how groups will be formed and where the groups can post messages and instructions on how to use any collaborative tools.

Although the major components of a face-to-face syllabus can be included in an online syllabus, the differences mentioned here must be included to reduce novice learners' anxiety of moving toward online learning. Encourage your learners to send e-mails or post comments in their introductions about syllabus concerns. You can also create a space in the "Coffee Table" section we mentioned earlier. This activity will begin learner-instructor, learner-learner, and learner-content interactions. It will also begin to develop trust and show that you can be responsive to learner concerns.

Create a "Start Here" or "Before You Begin" Space

This module in the content section provides the learners with an overview of the course as well as the policies and procedures that govern the conduct of the course. We have found that online students want structure in terms of course procedures, policies, and expectations. We also like to include an activity that enables students to navigate through the course site to build up their confidence in locating needed course materials. We also include an assignment that helps students try out the posting procedures as an introduction activity.

A new instructor suggested including a scavenger hunt (see Appendix H) so students would have to find certain materials located in different sections of the course. A scavenger hunt will let you know about the difficulties learners might have in the routes established for finding materials. This is also a good opportunity to fix any broken links.

On the "Before You Begin" page, we include four headings: "About the Course"; "About the Instructor"; "Navigating the Online Instructional Platform"; and "Instructional, Technical, and Support Services and Resources."

- "About the Course" informs the students of policies, procedures, expectations for postings, and the syllabus and describes how we will communicate, how we prepare and guide our communications (i.e., netiquette), and how we will begin to relate as a community of learners.
- "About the Instructor" tells the students about our practical and academic experience with the subject matter and begins to build our credibility as subject matter experts.
- "Navigation" links to help for the online instructional platform and provides guidance on what students will find in the different sections of the course, for example, content modules, discussion boards, and the dropbox area for sharing assignments.
- "Instructional, Technical, and Support Services" provides links and directions on how to obtain assistance with the online instructional platform, and how to access academic support services such as tutoring, writing assistance, and departmental assistance. Other support services might include links to the Office of Disability Services and the counseling center.

Introduce Yourselves

As noted previously, we use the introduction as a low-risk way to help students build confidence about navigating through the course site and trying out the posting process if they're new to our online instructional platform. More important, though, introductions help learners connect with others and with us and help establish a sense of community. The following contains what some former students suggest regarding introductions:

On the discussion board, you can guide the introductions with questions similar to ones you might use in a traditional classroom. Ask students about their background and their expectations for the course. Encourage students to post a picture. Ask your students how they prefer to learn. Finally, throw in some fun questions to create a social atmosphere and help people get to know each other!

Post Weekly Announcements

Communicate often and use the news section to post weekly announcements, thoughts that emerge from weekly activities, and upcoming events (which can also be posted in the calendar). We post a message before the course starts telling learners when the course site will become live. Later, we post a message reminding learners of the start date.

After the first week, we post a summary of the activities and insights learners might obtain from participating in the activities. We send the same information before the course starts to the learners by e-mail in case they are not checking the course site. Again, our purpose is to build a sense of excitement about the course and to demonstrate that even though we are at a distance, we are involved, thinking of our learners, and encouraging our learners to familiarize themselves with the tools and activities before the course officially begins.

Points to Remember

- Create a connection with each student and with the whole class.
- Provide the class with opportunities to explore the course site prior to the start of the class.
- Provide the class with the syllabus, policies, procedures, expectations, and opportunities to pose questions and express concerns.
- Learn about your students, and give your students the opportunity to learn about you and each other.
- Welcome the students to the e-classroom, which is a safe and inviting place to learn; provide reassurance that learning online works.

For Reflection

1. Read the sample welcome and expectations messages in Appendix G.
   a. Draft a welcome message and an expectations message for your course.
2. Read How to Develop a Scavenger Hunt in Appendix H.
   a. Reflect on the advantages and disadvantages of incorporating a scavenger hunt in your course.

FOURTH CHALLENGE

MANAGING AND FACILITATING THE ONLINE CLASSROOM

MANAGING AND FACILITATING THE ONLINE CLASSROOM

It was very interesting to work with a small group to analyze and discuss the questions and the readings. As group members contributed their perspectives, we built consensus and constructed our understanding of various aspects of adult education. It was a new process for me and it was a very engaging way to learn. In our whole-class face-to-face meetings, I enjoyed getting the wider perspectives of a larger group. I also liked hearing from the professors because of their expertise in the field.

—Joan, online learner

I did not think there was good participation on the discussion board each week. Especially as the quarter progressed, fewer people posted comments. Many comments were not posted until late Sunday night after I was immersed in the new readings and questions. There were a few people who always had insightful postings and added depth to the discussion. Some people recommended books or websites in their responses that expanded my thinking.

—Hilda, learner in same course as Joan

The more meaningful the participation in an online class, the greater the quality of the learning experience and the greater the overall satisfaction that learners have with being members of an online class. As we have previously mentioned, a worthwhile learning experience consists of social, teaching, and cognitive presence. Even in face-to-face classrooms, the three presences are necessary. The difference online is in how we think about and create the sense of presence. After completing this chapter, you will be able to do the following:

- Promote regular participation in class activities
- Use discussion boards to make thoughts visible

- Move discussions to higher levels
- Monitor participation and interactions with your class
- Analyze how to address student frustration

Teaching Presence

Teaching presence means that the course structure, facilitation, and direct instruction (content inputs) are designed to build cognitive presence (Anderson, Rourke, Archer, & Garrison, 2001). Although teaching presence is often thought to mean the teacher is present, in an online course we all have the responsibility for bringing in content, organizing our group (if we have groups), and helping each other understand the flow of the course. In a face-to-face course, and even online, we have a tendency to default to the instructor. If we are trying to build a community of learners, we all need to take responsibility for teaching presence.

With teaching presence, we engage with each other to help build individual and class understandings. We use chats and discussion boards to help learners see and hear the thoughts of others and to engage in higher order thinking. Think of teaching presence as the transmission component that allows us to set the pace, sequence, and activities that support and encourage students to work with materials and build their understanding of the content.

Teaching presence is the timing belt that helps us manage learners, the dialogue, and the conditions for learning. Teaching presence is also manifested in how we manage and respond to expected and unexpected events. As instructors, our role is to move learners to take on additional responsibilities for their own learning. Online, we are partners in helping each and all to have an understanding of the issue under study.

We do not advocate preparing 50-minute lectures as the sole manner of establishing teaching presence online. Let the materials you select and describe provide the content. Why invest time in presenting content that has been previously developed?

We suggest an online instructor manage a course by evaluating and selecting the best content available from subject matter experts, describing the material, providing direction on how to use the material, and guiding students through the material. In a blended mode or flipped classroom mode, face-to-face class time can be used to work with content perhaps in ways that cannot be accomplished online. Let the virtual classroom be the space for content acquisition, content creation, and sharing of thoughts.

> ### Insights From a New Online Instructor
>
> I am upfront with learners and tell them that they can't hide online. I know how often they log in, and I can see their contributions. I will contact them if they are missing from the course. Frankly, I never did that kind of outreach in courses I taught in person. Maybe I should have.

Five Ways to Manage and Facilitate Teaching Presence

You can manage and facilitate teaching presence in five ways: promote participation, share thoughts by employing group activities, participate in discussions, monitor participation and interactions with others, and stay involved.

Promote Participation

In the opening weeks of your course, establish the need for students to participate consistently online. This can be accomplished with your welcome letter and expectations message. You can also encourage consistent participation by communicating by e-mail with your students if participation is lacking. Allow for alternate means of submitting work, such as audio and video submissions.

During the beginning phases of your online course, it is important to establish your regular participation by checking the quality and quantity of responses in class activities and providing supporting material, such as additional readings, links, and new ideas to keep a discussion flowing. Telling learners about your participation can be accomplished with your welcome letter and expectations message. You can also encourage consistent participation on the part of your learners by communicating by e-mail if participation is lacking.

Zimmerman (2012) remarked that the more students touch course materials, the more likely their end-of-course performance will meet course goals. In our courses, we have used the Four Rs to increase content touchpoints in a discussion-based learning environment: read, reflect, respond, and revise (Padilla Rodriguez & Armellini, 2013). We develop a schedule showing how the instructional events will occur. Participants are expected to read the materials, reflect on their own meaning of the materials given a situation relevant to their world, respond to the class collaboration site and engage with the content posted by others, and revise their thinking, which we find is often neglected in discussion activities. Table 7.1 is an example of a discussion participation schedule for our learners.

TABLE 7.1
Discussion Participation Schedule

Date	Activity
March 22–24	Read materials in Module 6. Prepare your initial ideas for posting to the class.
March 25–26	Reflect on the meaning of the content and post your initial thoughts on the discussion board.
March 27–29	Respond to the threads in the whole-class discussion room. Engage with at least one class member. Start a new thread as new ideas emerge.
March 30	Revise your initial post based on comments received if your thoughts have changed. Label the post "Final Thoughts."

Employ Small-Group and Whole-Group Activities

Use the discussion board and other collaborative or sharing sites to make visible the thoughts of students and give students an opportunity to converse with peers about the meaning, application, and novel ways of dealing with course content. Through discussion, learners can actively participate daily in the course. However, without proper facilitation, discussions can become an oppressive learning technique, forcing students to make responses simply to meet a requirement. We used to think that learners had the skills to be discussants. After many discussion board experiences, we no longer assume that learners have the skills to conduct discussions efficiently, integrate information, and resolve issues under discussion. As online instructors, we encourage you to help organize discussion groups by having groups name a moderator and summarizer (the design and organization category of teaching presence); gain input from all (facilitating discourse category); and present questions, refer to readings, and summarize and check for everyone's understanding (direct instruction category).

Participate in Discussions

We have found it helpful to provide practice and coaching sessions before conducting a full discussion, including observing conversations, identifying process errors, and providing feedback (Stein & Wanstreet, 2013). We encourage you to participate in the discussions early in the course and early in the week. Be in the classroom, actively adding content, comments, and critique. We have seen online courses where only the learners are involved in the discussions. The instructor seems to take only the role of evaluator, grading discussions, assignments, and posting a weekly announcement. A learner in these courses might wonder where the instructor is. Although the instructor does respond to questions if asked, presence is very low. As a facilitator of an online course, your role is to move the discussion to higher levels by asking learners to clarify, expand on, explain, critique the content, and respectfully push other learners to see the assumptions behind their statements. As an instructor, you also have the responsibility to comment on postings that might have erroneous information. You might also start new threads based on ideas arising from the discussion boards. Waiting too long to post comments might result in a wandering discussion; coming in too soon may mean that you as instructor are dominating the discussion. From a student's perspective, consider whose remarks have more importance or weight—those from your colleagues or your instructors.

Although we do not want the instructor to dominate the discussion board—these discussions do belong to the students—we also do not want misinformation to be posted, nor do we want instructors to be absent. You can participate in discussions to promote higher order thinking in the following ways:

- Prompt learners to justify their responses by using the existing literature rather than providing only personal opinion.
- Promote engagement by asking students to acknowledge the contributions of others as a way of building ownership of their ideas.
- Push for ideas (statements) that go beyond the text and show originality in thinking.
- Encourage learners to share knowledge by having them bring in resources and readings beyond the required and recommended sources in the syllabus.
- Ask learners to connect content to real-world experiences and to provide relevant examples.

Monitor Participation and Interactions

You may find that students are not responding to discussion posts or participating in class activities. Students may respond but are not offering new thoughts or asking for clarification or expansion of the thoughts posted. During the beginning stages of your online course, you could ask yourself the following questions:

- Am I posting interesting and challenging questions that relate to the real concerns and lives of the students? Students who do not see the relevance of the question may be reluctant to post.

- Have I created a safe environment for students to take a risk? Students may not feel safe expressing their thoughts. Students may feel their thoughts are not worthy or would not be favorably received. Familiarize yourself with netiquette at www.albion.com/netiquette or a source of your choice. Post netiquette sites and establish group norms that promote an environment of trust and collaboration. Instructors can remind students of proper ways to respond and monitor critiques that are not helpful to the learning of the group.

- Am I modeling how I want students to participate? The instructor can model the type of responses required either in the form of a rubric or by taking part in the discussion. If students see that the instructor is present and commenting, this might motivate students to join in the discussion.

- Am I following up on nonresponders as soon as I notice the problem? For example, check the analytics of your course management system. If learners are not meeting deadlines, send them an e-mail. We recommend doing this the first time a student misses a posting date. This will let the student know that performance is required. The instructor can ask for a reason the response is late or not posted. Of course, this would be done in the spirit of helpfulness and concern. If the learner doesn't follow up with you, send a second e-mail to determine if the student intends to continue in the course. In the meantime, assign a zero grade for nonresponse. First, show concern, then provide support. Finally, you may need to contact the learner to develop a plan to get the learner back on track.

- Are the responses of students being acknowledged? We ensure that every student who posts receives at least one comment either from us or from other classmates. To help distribute responses, we have established a policy of asking students to not post to participants who have received at least two to three responses from other classmates. We have not found adequate justification to require a specific number of response posts. In our classes, we establish a minimum requirement for each participant to post to at least one other student. We have found that most students will exceed the minimum requirement because of their interest in the topic. Their curiosity about how their thoughts are received becomes a motivating factor.

Although we believe that working together can produce a thought that goes beyond what an individual can develop alone, we caution instructors not to overuse the collaborative discussion. Discussions can become just another type of assignment to be completed for a grade. Thus, we vary the pace of the course and mix individual activities with group discussions. With individual assignments, we provide an option for participants to comment on the work of others. In addition, we do not grade assignments other than on a satisfactory or unsatisfactory basis. Removing the idea of points for each post allows us to focus on the quality of the post.

Stay Involved

Remind students of classroom procedures and processes to keep the course moving on track. Provide a weekly summary of comments contributing to the overall understanding of content, and include your own thoughts regarding the issue. Use the news tool to bring closure to the module's activities and to introduce the upcoming learning activities. Provide personal feedback to every student at some time, and each week acknowledge what the class is doing.

A student said that one of the best online learning courses she had taken captured the spirit of teaching presence. Notice the importance of course design and delivery, facilitation, and direct instruction in her comment: "I appreciated the clear expectations, logical organization of the online environment, and examples provided of what deliverables might look like and opportunities to practice those deliverables. I also liked the practical application of ideas."

Just as students may become fatigued during a 16-week semester, so do we as instructors. To keep involved, we look for new tools that can be used to show learner mastery of the content. We ask the students to present their thoughts as posters, comic strips, or cartoon characters in a video or audio format. We find that our interest is maintained by learning a new tool and admiring the creativity learners show when presenting content.

Facilitating Group Work

A benefit of the Internet is the ability for a group of people to share ideas and build new knowledge together. The original design of the Internet was to allow researchers to expand their ability to think together. However, in the classroom setting, and especially in the virtual classroom, working together presents unique challenges. We have found that some students have an aversion to group work that carries over from the physical classroom. Unequal distribution of effort, members not participating or meeting deadlines, and the difficulties of arranging time and place for group members to meet will also arise in the online classroom. If learners have difficulties in a physical space, imagine their concerns about working together in virtual spaces. To promote more confidence in the group learning process and in collaborative work, we have used a sequential approach to build skills in learning together on line.

Moving Toward Collaborative Learning

We have learned to use low-risk tasks that are easy to accomplish. The first step is to move learners through individual postings to develop the idea that they can communicate in an electronic environment. The second step is paired dialogue in which learners post and respond to others in the classroom and practice sharing their thoughts. The third step, which comes at around the fifth week of a semester class, is small-group work with large-group sharing.

Spaces for Group Work

To increase comfort with learning together virtually, we provide collaboration spaces in our online instructional management system. We also permit learners to select their own platforms for meeting. Some have used Google tools for collaborative work or other spaces available online. To protect privacy we do not require learners to use third-party tools that require setting up an account. We also assign group members on a random basis to ensure that characteristics that might influence group discussions are equally distributed. We also note that by the fifth week of class, learners have interacted with a high percentage of classmates and have a basic knowledge of group members.

Develop a Charter

The first task is to develop a working peer-designed agreement for when to meet; how to meet; roles and responsibilities of group members; how to deal with absences because of family, work, or other life circumstances; what it means to come prepared to the group meeting; and how to handle conflict and other situations that might adversely affect the operation of the group. This activity begins to establish ownership of the group process. The agreement is posted in the small-group area where the instructors can monitor the group and suggest ways to enhance group functioning. An activity associated with this phase is to name the group. One of our former classes followed the following five-step discussion process:

1. Introduction: We introduced ourselves and talked about individual aspirations, areas of study, and our reasons for taking the course.
2. Listening: Listening was instituted in this initial process and throughout. As we prepared for the next week, we became aware of

adjustments that would have to be made to accommodate schedules. We each paid attention and made decisions accordingly.

3. Consideration: Common courtesy was evident by the ways in which we related to each other. These included conversations; for example, if interrupting or interjecting comment, there was an apology for doing so (even if it was a qualified interruption). Consideration was also shown by group members making necessary accommodations for each other. One member called me from work to make certain that our plans would proceed. Mutual respect and mutually validating each other's experiences as group members, I believe, made this a strong component. E-mails have also served an important purpose in furthering cooperation through courtesy.

4. Establishing a Safe Zone: In order for us to work effectively as a group, consideration demonstrated through courtesy allowed us to feel fairly comfortable in expressing some personal challenges (e.g., technophobia). It also opened the door for us to ask each other questions (eliciting more detail) or clarifying comments of conversation.

5. Roles of Group Communication Filled: The roles of group inter- action were filled in an easygoing and somewhat fluid manner. The person who volunteered to be the week's scribe functioned as initiator/ leader. The role, however, was passed around the table as each one had the opportunity to bring up additional points for consideration. We had a gate-keeper who looked (visually) to see what someone else may have had to offer that was evident by facial/nonverbal cues. At one point, there was a "hiccup" in the idea-generating portion, and the gate-keeper made a point of getting another member's input. The role of clarifier was played by everyone. This was a primary contribution to getting the depth of response from each person and the safety felt within the group environment.

Feedback or mirroring (responses) was a role several group members played. It often came from the one who was recording the information, but it was also subject to change if any individual member felt comfortable pro- viding feedback. (We differentiate this role from clarifying. Feedback or mir- roring is a simple restatement of what you heard in an effort for the sender to hear and affirm or for her or him to clarify.) Summarization was determined by the whole group in that each was highly focused and engaged in the pro- cess of what needed to be done within the time frame.

Notice the roles assigned to group members. Each member of the group takes a position to question, clarify, lead, and record the thoughts of the group. The moderator and recorder roles are fixed to ensure the completion of the task. We have found the role of moderator is critical in moving the group toward cognitive presence, and thus we provide additional training on how to be a moderator. The following list describes the group members' roles.

- Moderator: The moderator helps set norms, facilitates discussion, and connects ideas.
- Recorder: The recorder feeds the results of the discussion back to the group at appropriate points during the discussion, for example, by inserting, "Here's what we are saying as a group." At the end of the discussion, the recorder sends the summary of the discussion to the group and posts the final summary of the group's deliberation to the discussion board after getting input from the group members. The recorder's primary contribution to the discussion is to keep track of what all group members are saying.
- Everyone: All group members are responsible for supporting opinions with information from the readings.

Keeping Involved

Participants may still not be confident in the ability of their group to produce a high-quality discussion product, and we often receive comments about participation and how grading will be accomplished. Our response is to structure activities to relate to the working world where projects are not graded individually, and it is up to the members to complete the task even if some participants do not carry out all their responsibilities.

Here is a common situation described by a learner.

> I had group work in two classes—one face-to-face and another online. The online group lost a member immediately. As a whole, that group work was otherwise fine. The face-to-face class small group did not want to participate during the class time allotted to discussion, and what should have been simple exercises turned into a production at times. One of the members who helped facilitate our online posts dropped out of our group and the class without any notice. It is awkward at best to try and police fellow students and makes more work overall.

An advantage of a virtual group discussion is that we can monitor participation. Although we do not interfere in the group process, we do visit the chat rooms to gauge the quality and quantity of participation. If we notice that a member has not contributed, we send an e-mail to the member asking if there were any technical or other difficulties in accessing the space. If participation is still not forthcoming, we send another e-mail reminding the member of the charter as well as course expectations. If nonparticipation continues, the learner does not receive any credit for the activity. We do encourage participants to contact their group if a work or family commitment might interfere with actively contributing to the group. The following insight is from one of our learners:

> I think that the best way to improve classroom collaboration is through a mutual peer agreement. It is hard to keep track of all of the people and their schedules when working in a group. With a collective agreement about tasks and roles, every group member knows what work they need to complete and are not confused about what is expected. In our group, we struggled in this area because we were unsure about what each person was going to do. With some more conversation, this problem has greatly improved!

What Teaching Presence Means to Your Course

Managing and facilitating the online environment during the beginning of your class means that you

- organize discussion groups or study groups and provide direction;
- contribute to the discussion board by posing questions, acknowledging responses, and moving the conversation to higher levels of discourse;
- remind students of netiquette and classroom procedures and processes to keep the course moving on track and providing input appropriately;
- input knowledge in terms of content and additional resources and provide input in clarifying misconceptions; and
- encourage student engagement with others and the sharing of reasoned, critical thought.

In speaking with new online instructors, we note that being present is very important to keep students motivated and engaged with course content and with each other. The following case illustrates this point.

The Case of the Disgruntled Student

Professor Glazer was teaching a fully online philosophy of science course to first-year doctoral students. For many of the students, this was their first exposure to research and to the philosophical foundations of knowledge construction. The course was structured with readings, a short introduction to the concept for the week, and a discussion board. Each student was required to post a response concerning the subject matter. Each student was required to respond to at least two classmates. The instructor did provide group feedback to point out the strengths and weaknesses in the class responses, posed questions to advance the understanding, and provided content to further explain the concepts under study. In addition, feedback was provided to individual students showing how the response could be improved or letting the student know that the response posted did meet the criteria for an acceptable response.

During the first three weeks of the course, one student consistently posted information that did not demonstrate mastery of the concepts. The student sent an e-mail saying, "You are not teaching me anything. Where are your lectures? How am I supposed to learn this material?" Professor Glazer was stunned but responded to the student by e-mail explaining her position regarding online learning. Table 7.2 shows what happened next.

TABLE 7.2

Disgruntled Student Interactions

Student Comment	Instructor Response
Where are your lectures? How am I to learn the material if you do not teach it to me?	In an online course, individual and group feedback is used to improve individual performance.
Posting comments is not teaching.	Here is how to use the study notes, discussion board, and text material to assist your retention of the content response. When you have questions, e-mail me or post questions to the "Ask the Instructor" page.
I don't know how to learn this way.	You may want to consider visiting the academic services resource center to help with reading or comprehension issues.
If you don't teach, how am I supposed to learn?	The online learning process uses materials and short notes or lectures to expand and clarify your knowledge of the material by reading. This allows you to have more knowledge of the material. Reflecting on content in the discussion board allows you to make a thoughtful statement regarding the readings and to question the readings. Reading others' discussion posts helps you to see what other students are getting from the readings, perhaps something that you might have missed.

Insights From a New Online Instructor

I must model the behavior that is required. How I moderate the discussion will be important. I must show my constant presence, let them know that I am actually reading their responses. I can do this by providing occasional responses without dominating the discussion. My responses must be supportive and validating to encourage them, let them know they are in the right direction or help them get onto the right direction. I can offer questions to stimulate their thinking and move the discussion forward.

It is also important that I help the students understand the benefits of engaging in the discussion forum, how it helps them to check whether they understand the course material. I will also point out how they can benefit from the thinking of others, that they may get answers to questions that they themselves have. Their contributions to the discussion can count for part of their overall grade. That, I think, has to be done cautiously as I do not want them posting something simply for the grade.

Points to Remember

- Promote regular participation in class activities.
- Use the discussion boards to make the thoughts of students visible.
- Move discussions to higher levels by asking learners to clarify, expand on, explain, critique content, and respectfully push other learners to see the assumptions behind their statements.
- Monitor participation and interactions with others.
- Stay involved to keep the course moving on track.

For Reflection

1. Review Table 7.2 and reflect on the instructor's responses in the case of the disgruntled student. How would your responses differ?

FIFTH CHALLENGE

ASSESSING LEARNER
OUTCOMES

ASSESSING LEARNING IN
THE ONLINE CLASSROOM

I took a graduate online course. It was a complete disaster. The goal was to read the book and take online quizzes to test your knowledge. The questions were timed for 60 seconds, so you couldn't look up the answers in the book. After the quizzes, you were allowed to look at the questions and the right answers—which were actually incorrect in some cases. The professor told me it was just a glitch but wouldn't give me credit for having the right answer. I came away from the class with a very negative feeling about online courses.

—Annie, graduate student

I was in an online course that had timed tests over four or more chapters at a time. Needless to say, it was frustrating and I didn't gain much from the course. Instead of trying to get involved in the class, I ended up just doing what I could to pass and didn't try to actually learn. However, I also had an online class with lots of group discussions that allowed us to share our ideas and create new concepts from others. So I guess online courses really depend on the instructor and the class material.

—Joseph, graduate student

In previous chapters we discussed the importance of planned interaction to successful online learning. In this chapter, we discuss instructor-learner interaction through assessments. In the online environment, students lack the visual and verbal cues to show they are mastering the content and achieving the weekly objectives. Assessments are one feedback mechanism used to measure progress toward achieving instructional goals. This is a form of cognitive presence and completes the cycle of building a worthwhile learning experience. In this chapter we first present the general concept of assessment, followed by the types of assessments you might use in an online course. We conclude with situations you might encounter in the beginning phases of your online course. After completing this chapter, you will be able to do the following:

- Determine which type of feedback is appropriate for particular types of assignments
- Define *meaningful feedback*
- Explain how to use authentic assessments
- Formulate feedback for a late assignment
- Identify tools learners can use to demonstrate competence

Regular Feedback

Cognitive presence includes the intellectual skills of knowledge acquisition and application. It is the outcome factor in our model of online learning. At the end of each online session, week, or module, we recommend providing students with feedback that clearly indicates they are becoming more skilled in the content than before they began the lesson. During the beginning sessions of an online course, students may have doubts about whether their responses are meeting the intent of your assignments and whether they are acquiring the knowledge that is required to successfully master the weekly objectives.

Establishing a regular pattern for responding to student work will indicate to online learners that you are there reviewing and commenting on the performance of your students. Assessing student work on a predictable basis will provide opportunities for students to improve their performance. This is known as formative feedback, and it also helps you identify early in the course learner actions that might be detrimental to the overall course design, such as lack of participation or responses that lack depth of thought.

Levels of Learning and Assessments

Assessments are comparisons of student performance measured against course objectives. This is known as alignment. Your content should be related to the course objectives, which are met by the activities learners use to demonstrate levels of proficiency.

Assessment tools are related to levels of learning specified in your course syllabus. A popular tool for building learning assessments is Bloom's revised taxonomy (Anderson & Krathwohl, 2001). Assessments are linked to levels of learning. Look at your weekly learning objectives. Simple quizzes using matching or multiple-choice questions would be appropriate for demonstrating remembering content such as definitions or naming concepts or objects. To demonstrate understanding, short essays, one-minute papers, blogs, tweets, or individual posts on a discussion board would be appropriate tools to employ. To show that learners can apply content to a new situation, consider quizzes in the form of a scenario or producing a picture book or a cartoon.

Higher levels of learning involving analyzing, evaluating, and creating begin to move assessments from the individual learning levels to collaborative demonstrations of learning, and we move from objective to subjective forms of assessments. Subjective forms of assessments require a rubric to show learners what makes an acceptable response. Consider using case studies, simulations, or group projects that produce novel ways of working with content and perhaps even generate new content in the form of research papers and reflective discussion posts. Creating knowledge is usually the outcome of longer periods of time. However, it is possible using discussion boards and case studies, for example, to demonstrate analysis and evaluation in a weekly lesson or a module extending over a two-week period.

Assessment Through Rubrics

We are all familiar with quizzes, exams, and reports as assessment tools. In the first week we focus on a tool that may be unfamiliar to you. In setting expectations and in grading, one method for establishing criteria is the rubric. Typically, rubrics are developed for specific activities, such as essays or projects. But in online learning, the discussion or post is often added. This is particularly the case when one of the objectives is to improve critical thinking; it sets the standard for the learner. The purpose of using the rubric for grading is to quantify the way information is transmitted to the learner. We recommend setting up a rubric for every written assignment, such as papers, projects, and discussion boards. Elements that go into a discussion rubric, for example, might include

- content and focus,
- evidence of critical thinking,
- evidence of analysis and synthesis,
- logic and flow,
- structure and organization, and
- adherence to a style or format.

Grading might use the following schema: 5 = *strong*, 4 = *proficient*, 3 = *satisfactory*, 2 = *weak*, and 1 = *unacceptable*.

Using Feedback to Improve Performance

Feedback is an essential component of online teaching. The quotes at the beginning of the chapter show that students expect the voice of the instructor to be there throughout the course. Hearing from the instructor is preferred over objective means of assessing performance. Feedback provides students with an understanding of the instructor's expectations, their own comprehension, and areas in which they can improve.

Providing feedback is important, and the quality, timing, and relevance of feedback are equally essential. With no feedback or feedback that is unclear, irrelevant, belittling, or late, students often feel frustrated and confused. Feedback is provided through e-mails, comments on assignments, and most often in discussion boards. Statements provided by instructors can be categorized as supportive, informational, corrective or confirming, procedural, and inquiring.

> ### Insights From a New Online Instructor
>
> Students want to see that the instructor cares about them. This can be achieved through timely feedback of assignments, through challenging their critical thinking on discussion boards as well as responding to their questions and e-mails promptly.

Supportive feedback. Supportive feedback identifies with the emotions expressed in a posting. It is an acknowledgment that learners might be having difficulties or have reached a breakthrough or that perhaps life gets in the way of meeting deadlines.

Informational feedback. Informational feedback introduces resources or ideas that may help the learner move to higher levels of thinking.

Corrective or confirming feedback. Corrective or confirming feedback is used to show errors in thinking or misinformation. A corrective feedback statement also provides guidance on how to correct performance. Confirming feedback shows the learner that performance is meeting or exceeding the standards. "Good work" is not an acceptable form of feedback. State why the work is good.

Procedural feedback. Procedural feedback provides guidance on course procedures, such as due dates. Administrative feedback clarifies course requirements and instructor expectations.

Inquiring feedback. Inquiring feedback is most often used in discussion boards to push students to further explain, challenge, and consider alternative points of view. It is the voice of the instructor prompting the learners to exhibit deeper learning. In our courses, we use the following statements when we ask learners to provide inquiring feedback to their colleagues in a discussion board:

> To receive a satisfactory grade for the discussion, your initial posting must meet the following criteria:
>
> - Your assertions should show evidence and support from the readings and other course materials.
> - Your initial posting should refer to the postings of at least two other colleagues.
> - Your posting should show how it is supporting previously stated positions, challenging those positions, or adding a new idea to the discussion.
> - Your response post should show how it helps expand the thinking of the colleague to whom you are responding by asking for clarification or expansion, querying an assumption or assertion, using a counter-argument, or asking for an illustration or more precise details.

Learner Self-Assessments and Reactions

As an online instructor, you will not often have the opportunity to gauge the reaction of your students to instruction. How will you know if the learners are bored, excited, confused, or enlightened by the online learning experience? Each learner will have a different reaction to your teaching style and to the content presented.

Questions include the following: How in a class of online learners can I know the emotional and intellectual reactions that are occurring in every class session? How can I get learners to honestly share with me their thoughts about the content, my approach to the content, the activities I am using, and the overall climate of the classroom?

Stephen Brookfield (2011) suggests that at regular intervals and sometimes after every class session, classroom reaction tools are available to help you estimate how instruction and learning are happening. Three tools that would be appropriate for your learners include the Muddiest Point (i.e., asking learners what was most confusing), the Learning Audit (i.e., asking learners what they know now that they didn't know before), and the Classroom Critical Incident Questionnaire (available from www.stephenbrookfield .com/ciq).

Those tools are designed for learners to share how they are thinking and feeling about the session with the instructor in an anonymous manner. The depth of responses is a factor of the trust that exists between you and the learners as well as your commitment to act on those aspects of your teaching that might need improvement. There may be aspects of your classroom that you value and that define you as a teacher. For example, we do not believe in long video lectures; however, we would modify our approach if the openness of the classroom was not helping the learners at all. We would try different activities without giving a full three-hour presentation.

The Muddiest Point, Learning Audit, and Critical Incident Question-naire tools not only provide feedback to you but also encourage the learners to become more reflective about how they are presenting themselves in the classroom environment and how they are internally being responsive to the classroom situation. End-of-course assessments do not help us correct and improve our skills or make adjustments to help students learn. The use of the classroom reaction tools provides continuous guidance on how students, think, feel, and act in our instructional settings.

An instructor who notices that students are either not participating in online activities or performing only at minimal standards can provide feed-back at the individual and class level. Inadequate performance might be indicative of content that is not related to the real-world experiences or con-cerns of the student, lack of motivation or interest in the content on the part of the student, lack of confidence in one's ability to participate in meaningful ways (nothing valuable to say), or pressing life demands that make it difficult to participate online.

Gathering information using the Muddiest Point, Learning Audit, and Critical Incident Questionnaire tools can help you and your students have a more positive online experience. In our courses, if we see students not participating in any given week, we send an e-mail inquiring about their circumstances. This shows the student that you are concerned and that the student's absence is noticed.

Evaluations and FERPA Guidelines

You'll want to become familiar with the Family Educational Rights and Privacy Act (FERPA, 1974), which was designed to protect the privacy of stu-dents by establishing conditions for use and release of information. Hillison, Pacini, and Williams (2000) offer guidance to instructors and administrators regarding electronic storage and transmission of student records, including posting grades only on a secure system that ensures FERPA is not violated.

If you are not familiar with FERPA, review the FERPA guidelines at www2.ed.gov/ferpa as you think about how best to store and transmit assessment information.

Five Assessment Practices

The following are five assessment practices to use during the first few weeks of your course.

Assess Work Weekly

Provide formative assessments by including an assessment tool in every module related to the weekly objectives beginning with the first module or first week assignment. Using a weekly assessment tool shows students immediately how they are performing and where improvements might be necessary. Weekly assessments can keep students involved with the course and continue to build learner-content and learner-instructor interactions. Students who can see incremental building of content knowledge may be more likely to persist in the online course.

Post Grades Weekly

Post grades each week with feedback on the student's performance. Feedback can be posted either on the discussion board or in the dropbox. We prefer to have assignments posted in the dropbox. This will provide you with an organized way to collect assignments and provide feedback. Feedback in the discussion board is at the group level. Corrective and confirmatory feedback is sent via private communications directly to the individual.

Provide Meaningful Feedback

Even if you are tired or bored with reading the same responses over and over, provide feedback that is meaningful, pointing out the strengths in a response as well as how to improve areas where a student might be weak. Remember how Annie perceived the instructor at the beginning of this chapter. Start strong by providing feedback during the first week of the class and continue to provide feedback on a timely basis as the course proceeds.

Use Authentic Assessments

Build assessments that are authentic. Objective tests as well as discussion questions should relate to current issues of interest to students, be framed around situations learners are likely to encounter in their daily lives, and based on a combination of academic content and real-world problems. Assessments that are authentic can serve to build learner motivation and also measure the ability of the learner to apply the content in situations likely to be encountered.

Give Every Student Feedback

Provide feedback to every student during the first week of your online class. Use an assessment tool that will enable you to respond to each student as soon as the assignment is completed. Allow students to resubmit work that does not meet the standard. Responding to student work will show that you are assisting in the development of cognitive presence and providing an opportunity for students to better understand the tools as well as your expectations. In the second and subsequent weeks try to provide personal feedback to at least 10% of your learners. Over time, every learner will have an opportunity to receive a personal message.

Group Self-Assessment

Those who research the quality of online discussions generally suggest that the instructor is the major source of feedback and is primarily responsible for learner satisfaction with the experience (Nandi, Hamilton, & Harland, 2012). However, we suggest that learners themselves can be responsible for providing feedback to one another to determine if deep learning is taking place (Stein & Wanstreet, 2015). To that end, we have developed a peer-assessment rubric for use in learner-led online synchronous discussions that addresses the extent to which the group members' response to the discussion prompt meets the following criteria:

- Addresses the issue or problem
- Demonstrates use of evidence to support an argument
- Builds new ideas
- Indicates an awareness of the issue's context in the real world
- Shows mindful engagement among group members
- Is based on an analysis of multiple perspectives
- Shows analysis of evidence to arrive at a mutual understanding
- Shows sharing of personal insights and stories to provide a framework for the group's resolution

We coach our learners in how to use the peer-assessment rubric before their first online synchronous discussion, and group members have reported its usefulness in helping to keep the discussion focused on a resolution.

Points to Remember

- Assess work weekly to show students how they are performing and where improvements might be necessary.
- Post grades each week with feedback on the student's performance.
- Provide feedback that is meaningful, pointing out the strengths as well as areas in need of improvement.
- Use authentic assessments based on a combination of academic content and real-world problems.
- Provide feedback to every student during the first week of your class.

For Reflection

1. A learner in your course is a pastor who has written the following e-mail: "Dear Professor, I am writing to share with you what has happened this week. Early in the week, as I was working on the Unit 10 assignment, I began getting sick with a sinus infection. I went to the doctor to try to stave off the infection. At the same time I received a call from a parishioner that her brother-in-law passed away. After consoling the family, I went home and tried to recuperate. The next day, her husband died. I was with the family minutes after he passed, and needless to say it was and is a tough time. In the meantime, the sinus infection continued to worsen even on antibiotics, so much so that I was unable to perform the funeral service for the second man who passed away. With that said, I will be turning in Unit 10 late. I am sorry for this, but under the circumstances I have been unable to finish as I had previously planned. My goal is to turn the assignment in by Wednesday of this week. I know there will be some repercussions to the lateness of the assignment, but I wanted you to know what had happened to me this week. Being on call 24/7 has its challenges, and it seems the challenges get worse when an assignment is due. I am sorry for the delay."
   a. How would you respond to this learner?
   b. What effect does your institution's policy on late assignments have on your response?
   c. What elements besides your institution's policy on late assignments would you take into consideration in your response to this learner?

2. Review the tools that support Bloom's revised taxonomy at www.schrock guide.net/bloomin-apps.html. Notice the tools that can be used by learners to demonstrate competencies.

   a. What level of learning and what assessments might you use in the beginning of your course to build learner confidence and show that learning can happen in an online environment?

9

REFLECTING ON YOUR EXPERIENCE

If you have completed the challenges encountered in this text, you are ready to become an online teacher by adapting and adopting the thinking and practices of those who teach online.

You are now ready to master the challenges of the beginning weeks of your online course. The skills you have demonstrated in building social, teaching, and cognitive presence, which are the elements of a worthwhile learning experience, will also guide your practices throughout your course. The tool kit located in Appendix I describes practices and resources compiled by previous learners. We hope you find their suggestions valuable in teaching your own courses. You are now part of those of us who truly believe that networked Web-based learning represents a departure from the ways we teach and learn in the twenty-first century.

Becoming an online instructor takes practice, reflection on your practice, and continuous improvement of your practice. Becoming an online instructor means striving for excellence in this mode of instruction. Palloff and Pratt (2011) list the following characteristics of an excellent online instructor:

- Understands the unique characteristics of online instruction and uses the affordances to build interactive learning environments
- Supports and is committed to improving online instruction as a emerging form of teaching
- Establishes presence at the beginning of a course
- Builds community through social presence and realizes the necessity for social as well as task-focused conversations
- Continues to seek ways to build learner-learner, learner-instructor, learner-content, and learner-technology interactions

- Is actively engaged throughout the course, providing feedback to improve the quality and level of critical thinking and attainment of course goals
- Becomes a partner with the learners in developing content, providing resources, guiding the learning, and sustaining high levels of motivation (pp. 13–14)

Your understanding of the ideas in this text has equipped you to begin and continue your journey toward online teaching excellence. We hope you will include appropriate interactive elements in the courses you are assigned to teach. If your courses are already developed, look for ways to add elements that will enhance your interactions with learners. Continue to read and study the literature on practices in online learning.

The virtual classroom is becoming a major feature of learning in higher education. Universities are thought to have been stable learning organizations, slow to react to changing technologies. The idea of traditional learner-faculty interactions is the image of the philosopher flanked by a small group of students receiving wisdom. Yet that image is not true to the innovations that have changed the way many learners and teachers interact. Even in the Socratic dialogues, the role of the instructor was to challenge, push, and improve the critical and reflective thought process using the dialogic process. Certainly, the printing press provided alternative viewpoints to those argued by the master instructor. The development of mass instruction through the publicly supported school democratized learning and required new technologies to reach and engage large numbers of students. However, the skills of instruction may not have changed as dramatically as the technology used to support instruction.

Higher education learning environments are blending physical and virtual instruction to produce the flipped classroom, the hybrid classroom, the virtual classroom, and other forms that will emerge as technology continues to develop. Learners and teachers are connected through electronic tools as well as in physical space. Information is everywhere and is accessible immediately.

The classroom as we presently think of it, a physical space used for a single learning encounter, is and will become outdated. Learning sessions will be global, available any time and any place, to anyone who has access to the technology. What happens to the classroom when we escape the physical and electronic walls? What do learning and teaching look like when we enter a networked space that is mobile, learner controlled, learner centered, and always connected?

We believe that e-learning is the movement that provides learners with the means to take charge of their learning, to become connected and interdependent learners. E-learning may change the role of universities from being repositories of knowledge available to a privileged few to hubs connecting those who can share and those who are in need of knowing worldwide, anywhere, any place, any time, and with anyone. We welcome you to this exciting frontier, and we challenge you to bring forth new ideas and new ways of being an online teacher.

For Reflection

1. Complete again the Beginning Online Instructor Competencies and the Attitude Toward Online Teaching questionnaires.
   a. To what extent have your scores changed?
   b. In what area did you observe the biggest change? To what do you attribute this change?
2. Explore the tool kit in Appendix I.
   a. What insights did the contributions of previous learners provide?

10

CHALLENGE FOR THE FUTURE

Building Knowledge

In our discussions, we went back and forth gathering information, commenting on contributions, and putting our thoughts together. We went back and forth, back and forth, and it worked. . . . We just rocked.

—Michael, graduate student

People from different disciplines tend to do things differently. When you have a discussion with them, you learn from that and appreciate other people's point of view.

—Pat, new online instructor

Earlier we shared our insights about the importance of knowledge building in developing our philosophy of online instruction. In this chapter, we expand on the idea of knowledge building as a future challenge for online teaching and learning. We describe our knowledge-building process, our learners' perceptions of how they participated in an online collaborative learning experience in courses with knowledge building as the outcome, and recommendations for practice. This chapter will be more meaningful for you after you have completed the five challenges for new online instructors and have had some time to reflect on your teaching experience.

Knowledge building is a dynamic process formed on previous work, yet we as instructors tend to ignore the information products developed by students in previous iterations of our classes. Instead of using the previous work as a basis for the next class, we tend to begin each class at the same place. In the future, we should try to keep the information products growing. Students should be thinking about how the things they do will advance the understanding of the rest of the groups coming through the next class. In that way, they build a literature of the class, supported by wikis and other

Web collaborative tools, which will be used to develop and ultimately leave an information artifact.

For groups to generate knowledge, they must engage in knowledge building around inquiry rather than in knowledge acquisition and retention. For us, this means that discussions are critical to the success of inquiry-based learning.

Building Knowledge Through Discussion

Discussion is used as a collaborative activity to help learners become critically informed about a topic or issue, take responsibility for their learning, question their assumptions, and gain more insight into themselves as learners (Brookfield & Preskill, 2005). However, we have observed, particularly in asynchronous modes, that postings generally reflect an initial individual comment, and a response post may offer guidance and critique but might not change the original post or lead to new insights. Even in synchronous chats, students sometimes find that their group's discussion was more painful than productive (Stein & Wanstreet, 2013). To decrease the pain of shallow or poorly facilitated chats involves awareness on the part of the instructor about how learners can encourage discussion, coalesce as a group, and synthesize comments to move the group toward shared understanding (Stein et al., 2007).

The content posted in a discussion board is often not really a discussion but an exchange of information in a single direction, typically from the learner to the instructor with others observing the information (Chen & Wang, 2009). What is called discussion might be simply an exchange of individual ideas at best. In conversation, ideas and feelings are exchanged in a social, cooperative way. However, in a discussion, the intent is to push participants beyond their everyday thinking, to create a tension, and to produce a new and better understanding—a change in the way an issue is thought about. Discussion that produces improved understanding has the characteristics of mutual trust, respect for the members and members' contributions, and participants who demonstrate a willingness to listen and who are respectful of challenges to prevailing views. The work of a discussion is to make new meanings in a collective sense involving critical reflection on the premises of the arguments being formed.

Discussion can be a transformative experience when conducted in a democratic manner. In a democratic discussion, participants feel welcome, are receptive to new ideas and perspectives, participate in ways that are related to the issue under discussion, speak tactfully, express appreciation for thoughtful comments and insights, offer arguments and counterarguments supported by evidence, and are committed to the development of group learning (Brookfield & Preskill, 2005). The outcome of a discussion conducted in a democratic manner is new knowledge.

Garrison (2011) defines *inquiry-based discussions* as those in which learners take responsibility for their learning, create meaning in a group, and learn from the group using the democratic and ideal practices outlined by Brookfield and Preskill (2005) and Mezirow (1991). Garrison characterizes successful discussions as featuring learners engaged in purposeful, critical dialogue to construct individual and group understanding of an issue.

In online environments, Dennen (2008) notes that, at the very least, discussions may reduce isolation and provide a sense of connection to other learners. Beyond that, however, discussion can help move learners from independent thinking to interdependence, going beyond their present understandings to create new and refined knowledge constructions.

Knowledge-Building Process and Perceptions

We have developed a knowledge-building process based on the literature, our experiences facilitating online discussions, and on interviews with learners in our inquiry-based courses (Stein, Wanstreet, & Glazer, 2011). We discerned that building knowledge collaboratively involves six stages: committing to learn, becoming ready to participate, connecting to collaborate, achieving shared understanding, seeking community review, and making knowledge claims (see Figure 10.1). During the knowledge-building process, learners move from seeing themselves as individuals to identifying themselves as part of a group and becoming part of a larger learning community. The instructor's role is to provide coaching in content and in the knowledge-building process.

Stage 1: Commit to Learn

Committing to learn involves coming to the learning experience mindfully and establishing relationships with group members. Mindfulness involves the willingness to apply cognitive energy to engage with the thoughts of

Figure 10.1. The knowledge-building process.

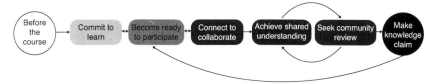

others, looking beyond the obvious, and responding with vigor and rigor (Langer, 1997). Learners who trust one another to work together can move to the next stage, becoming ready to participate.

Stage 2: Become Ready to Participate

The foundation of the collaborative knowledge-building process is the group members' readiness to participate (Lock, 2002). Learners become ready to participate by creating a welcoming climate, feeling emotionally and cognitively comfortable, and formulating initial thoughts on the discussion topic. Readiness to participate is reflected in the willingness of group members to get to know the course material in a way that supports collaborative learning. Being unprepared, uncomfortable, or noninclusive hinders participation and the ability of the group to achieve an understanding of the content that is shared by all. On the other hand, formulating initial thoughts in advance of the discussion contribute to learners' preparedness and ultimate satisfaction with the knowledge-building process.

Stage 3: Connect to Collaborate

Connecting to collaborate is dialogue that supports a knowledge-building experience. Learners connect to collaborate by brainstorming, exploring all points of view, challenging perceptions, ensuring equality of voices, and stretching individual perspectives to embrace others' perspectives. Brainstorming and exploring all points of view are ways of connecting to collaborate that help group members stretch their perspectives. Learning is strengthened through interactions that challenge their viewpoints. A challenge without empathy can be interpreted as rudeness and damage the climate for collaboration. Learners who are not willing to explore all points of view engage in shallow discussions that do not lead to shared understanding and knowledge building.

Stage 4: Achieve Shared Understanding

Achieving shared understanding results in a new perspective that did not exist before the group's discussion, which the group members come to accept as their new position and meaning. Establishing a collaborative environment that leads to shared understanding requires ample dialogue that connects group members with one another to explore and understand various perspectives deeply (Stein et al., 2007). Shared understanding is the result of knowledge building. Achieving shared understanding is difficult to do in a classroom situation with contrived groups of learners who may not be committed to collaborating.

Stage 5: Seek Community Review

Seeking community review is similar to the vetting process in academic publishing or in communities of practice. The community asks whether the work adds to the canon of knowledge, is novel, includes relevant prior work, presents information clearly, and makes reasonable and supportable claims.

Stage 6: Make Knowledge Claim

Making knowledge claims results from the community's review. A knowledge claim pushes the group's understanding about an issue beyond the existing published knowledge. A knowledge claim is a way to understand an issue that improves on earlier ways of understanding and can contribute to the learning of another group.

Recommendations for Practice

The promise of knowledge building lies in its dual capability to support the collective learning of future learners by building on the information artifacts produced by present learners and improving on what is known about a subject. Electronic tools for sharing emerging thoughts facilitate knowledge building and expand its reach outside the immediate classroom. However, the mind-set of instructors and the learners more than the technology is what helps or hampers the knowledge-building process.

To help students move from repeating what is known to creating and testing new ideas, refer to our collaborative knowledge-building framework that accounts for participation, collaboration, and shared understanding. Becoming ready to participate in collaborative knowledge building is the foundation of the framework and involves climate setting, establishing relationships, feeling emotionally and cognitively comfortable, and formulating initial thoughts on the discussion topic. Connecting to collaborate is achieved by brainstorming, exploring all points of view, challenging perceptions, ensuring equality of voices, and stretching individual perspectives to embrace others' perspectives. Shared understanding is individual and collective ownership of a new perspective accepted by the group. The struggle with trying to build online learning communities is in the difficulty of generating knowledge with an artificial classroom situation, time constraints, and a lack of commitment to the ideas of progressive discourse.

Learners in some classrooms may be more concerned with sharing information rather than with adding to the existing content in the field. To assist the knowledge-building process, consider conducting discussions on the idea of commitment when setting norms, including working toward mutual understanding, framing arguments in ways that can be supported by evidence, expanding the scope of propositions the group considers valid, and being open to critically examining any stance that will advance the discussion (Bereiter, 1994). Help learners understand that they each play a part in one another's learning, not only within their group but also within interlocking groups in the class. In that way, knowledge building will support the collective learning of the present group as well as that of future students.

APPENDICES

Appendix A: Beginning Online Instructor Competencies Questionnaire

Appendix B: Attitude Toward Online Teaching Questionnaire

Appendix C: Communication Plan Template

Appendix D: Communication Plan Checklist

Appendix E: Time Management Plan Checklist

Appendix F: Technology Tools

Appendix G: Sample Welcome and Expectations Messages

Appendix H: How to Develop a Scavenger Hunt

Appendix I: Tool Kit for Online Instructors

Beginning Online Instructor Competencies Questionnaire

The following is a list of competencies for instructors new to online environments. Competencies are expected knowledge, skills, and behaviors of instructors who teach online. Please indicate your level of competence by rating the following statements. Use the following code:

0 = I do not know anything about this topic.

1 = I have conceptual knowledge of this idea (I know what to do but have not done it).

2 = I have experiential knowledge of this competency (I have done this but don't know the concepts or theory).

3 = I have conceptual and experiential knowledge of this competency.

Task	Competency	Scale
Preparing Yourself to Teach Online		
	Understand time and space differences in online classrooms compared to face-to-face classes.	0 1 2 3
	Build interaction and feedback into each online meeting.	0 1 2 3
	Apply knowledge about copyright and legal issues when selecting and distributing online content. Assess learning materials for translation to an online environment.	0 1 2 3
	Set online office hours.	0 1 2 3
	Develop a communication plan for interactions with learners.	0 1 2 3
	Develop or adapt instructional materials for an online environment.	0 1 2 3
	Develop a syllabus with information specific to an online environment.	0 1 2 3
Selecting Appropriate Tools		0 1 2 3
	Navigate through the spaces in the online instructional platform.	0 1 2 3

Task	Competency	Scale
	Build discussion spaces; for example, Ask the Instructor, or collaborative or group spaces.	0 1 2 3
	Use the learner assessment features of the online instructional platform.	0 1 2 3
	Understand different delivery modes; for example, blended, synchronous, and asynchronous and the types of interaction each mode promotes.	0 1 2 3
	Use tools that support collaboration and individual work.	0 1 2 3
	Select tools within (or outside) the online instructional platform.	0 1 2 3
	Locate resources for technology support.	0 1 2 3
Preparing Learners to Learn Online		
	Establish expectations for learners and the instructor.	0 1 2 3
	Establish appropriate communication norms.	0 1 2 3
	Help learners become acclimated to the online instructional platform; e.g., navigation scavenger hunt.	0 1 2 3
	Create space and activities to develop a class identity.	0 1 2 3
	Help students gain confidence in learning online (low-risk assignments).	0 1 2 3
Facilitating Online Learning		
	Send a welcome message.	0 1 2 3
	Create a post-and-response routine.	0 1 2 3
	Address learner issues and other barriers that detract from learning.	0 1 2 3
	Respond to discussion postings and assignments in a timely fashion.	0 1 2 3
	Encourage participation.	0 1 2 3
	Ask questions and invite responses.	0 1 2 3
	Sustain engagement.	0 1 2 3
	Promote equality of voices.	0 1 2 3
	Provide coaching.	0 1 2 3
	Provide feedback.	0 1 2 3
	Motivate students via positive attitudes.	0 1 2 3
	Assess performance.	0 1 2 3

Task	Competency	Scale
	Make revisions to your course based on student feedback and instructor reflection.	0 1 2 3
Conducting Meaningful Appraisals of Student Learning		
	Create an online rubric that assesses higher-order thinking skills.	0 1 2 3
	Create an online quiz or exam.	0 1 2 3
	Create discussion questions that invite dialogue.	0 1 2 3
	Provide corrective, supportive, confirming, and informational feedback on assignments and postings.	0 1 2 3
	Write guidance describing rationale for assignments, including the grading criteria.	0 1 2 3

Attitude Toward Online Teaching Questionnaire

Indicate the extent to which you agree or disagree with the following statements. Use the following code:

1 = strongly disagree
2 = disagree
3 = neutral
4 = disagree
5 = strongly agree

Statement	Scale
1. Online education can be as effective in helping students learn as in-person instruction.	1 2 3 4 5
2. Effective digital tools are available to assess the quality of student learning online.	1 2 3 4 5
3. Online teachers connect with students well.	1 2 3 4 5
4. Instructors can build trusting relationships with students online.	1 2 3 4 5
5. My subject matter can be taught as well online as it can in person.	1 2 3 4 5
6. I get to know my students as well online as I do in person.	1 2 3 4 5
7. I am comfortable with the idea of teaching online.	1 2 3 4 5
8. I can easily help students solve learning problems.	1 2 3 4 5
9. I work harder and longer when teaching online compared with teaching face-to-face.	1 2 3 4 5
10. I feel that I will be able to communicate my subject matter online.	1 2 3 4 5
11. Students learn better when material is delivered online.	1 2 3 4 5
12. Learning outcomes in online education are inferior to outcomes in face-to-face instruction.	1 2 3 4 5
13. Online courses have higher dropout rates than face-to-face courses.	1 2 3 4 5

Communication Plan Template

1. E-mail: State when and why you will use this tool.

2. News or announcement page: State when and why you will use this tool.

3. Course calendar: State when and why you will use this tool.

4. Discussion boards: State when and why you will use this tool.

5. Web chats, including Skype, Adobe Connect, and/or other synchronous tools: State when and why you will use this tool.

6. Blogs: State when and why you will use this tool.

7. Social media sites: State when and why you will use this tool.

8. Other (please list): State when and why you will use this tool.

Communication Plan Checklist

U se this checklist as a guide to develop a communication plan.

Criterion	Yes	No
Minimum response times are specified.		
Regular time to be in the course is specified.		
Acceptable methods of communication are addressed (i.e., e-mail, IM, chat).		
Plan is defined for instructor.		
Plan is defined for students.		
Plan balances online time with regular life schedule.		
Plan helps to define your online persona.		

Time Management Plan Checklist

Use this checklist as a guide to develop a time management plan.

Criterion	Yes	No
The plan outlines a predictable presence in class.		
The plan defines assignment due dates and times.		
The plan defines when new content is posted.		
The plan defines when grades are reported.		
The plan defines when weekly, unit, and module summaries are posted.		
The plan contains or uses a course calendar.		
The plan allows for separation and balance of online course time and regular life schedules.		

Technology Tools

One of the challenges you will face as an online instructor is continually changing technology options that can aid you in reaching your students effectively. Employees of different institutions and organizations will have different resources at their fingertips; therefore, it is beneficial to have a list of free or low-cost tools. Keep in mind that it is always important to review terms and conditions of any programs or software you intend to use.

The following list was developed by Caryn Filson, Laura Kohlhorst-Jones, Jamie McConnell, Jamie Seger, and Heather Usher, all former students who gave permission for their list to be printed here.

Audio Recording and Editing

Audacity: audacity.sourceforge.net

Avatars

Voki: www.voki.com

Images (Editing)

GIMP: www.gimp.org
Google Photos Editor: support.google.com/photos/answer/6128850?hl=en
Paint.NET: www.getpaint.net

Images (Locating)

Clipart ETC: etc.usf.edu/clipart
Creative Commons: search.creativecommons.org
Flickr: www.flickr.com
Google Image Search: www.google.com/imghp
PicFindr: www.picfindr.com

Podcasts

Audacity: sourceforge.net/projects/audacity
Podomatic: podomatic.com
WinLAME: winlame.sourceforge.net

Polls, Surveys, and Quizzes

Polldaddy: www.polldaddy.com
Poll Everywhere: www.polleverywhere.com
Quiz School: www.proprofs.com/quiz-school
SurveyMonkey: www.surveymonkey.com

Screen Capture, Screen Casting

Screencast-O-Matic: www.screencast-o-matic.com
Jing: www.techsmith.com/jing.html

Slideshows (Narrated)

Microsoft PowerPoint: record narration option
Slideshare: www.slideshare.net

Video

YouTube: www.youtube.com
TeacherTube: www.teachertube.com
Vimeo: www.vimeo.com
Viddler: www.viddler.com

Web Page Editing

KompoZer: www.kompozer.net
Sea Monkey Composer: www.seamonkey-project.org

Sample Welcome and Expectations Messages

Sample Welcome Message

Dear Class:

Welcome to [insert course name]. This course will be completely online, and we will be communicating mainly through [insert name of course management system] and e-mail. This document discusses the nature of the learning environment I hope to create for this course, course rules and etiquette, expectations I have for the course work, and my role as the professor.

Throughout this course I hope to create and maintain a positive and collaborative learning environment. Our learning space should allow for commenting on others' work; while constructive criticism is encouraged, please also mention positive points in your peers' work. Having the ability to have your work viewed by your peers is rare; take advantage of it!

General Information

We will be using [insert name of course management system] for all of the instructional content, assignments, and assessments. If you are unfamiliar with [insert name of online instructional platform], you can use Help for Students to answer any questions you may have. Other resources can be found under Content in Course Resources. Please see the syllabus for guidance on assignments, deadlines, expectations and where to find additional support if needed. You will find these documents as well as my expectations for participating in this class in the Before You Begin module located in the content section of our course.

Because you are in an online course, it is imperative that you regularly check the course site (i.e., at least every two days) to stay abreast of new material and postings. In addition, to meet the learning goals and to receive timely feedback from the instructor, it is important that you complete assignments (including discussion postings) by the specified dates. If special circumstances arise that impact your ability to complete assignments (e.g., a summer storm wipes out power for several days), please contact me via e-mail [insert] or phone [insert].

You can look to me to answer questions you may have. However, it will be beneficial to you and your peers to post your questions on the discussion board for everyone to view and answer. I will review all posts and submit correct answers if needed. I will always try to return your graded work to you by the beginning of the following week so you are able to review it and use my feedback in the following week's assignments.

The grading scale is covered in the syllabus. I will hold virtual and face-to-face office hours on Monday and Thursday from 4:00 p.m. until 6:00 p.m. You can expect that I will review and respond to all questions in the Questions for Instructor discussion board in a timely manner. If you have more pressing needs or private questions during the course, feel free to e-mail me. I will respond to all e-mails within 24 to 48 hours.

How to Begin

Let's get to know each other and the course. First, read the materials in the Before You Begin module located in the content section of our course. Second, locate the Introduction assignment under Discussions. This assignment should be completed by Sunday, July 15, at 11:59 p.m.

Sample Expectations Message

Dear Learners,

This message explains my expectations for the course. Please feel free to respond to this message with questions or comments as they occur to you. The online teaching and learning process is a reciprocal relationship in which you take a majority of the responsibility for your learning. We work together to develop a vibrant learning community.

What is the grading scheme for this course?

- To earn a grade of A you have to demonstrate mastery in all projects and exceed expectations as defined in the scoring guide.
- To earn a grade of B you have to demonstrate proficiency in all projects and meet expectations for participation as defined in the scoring guide.
- To earn a grade of C you have to demonstrate limited proficiency in all projects and meet half of the expectations for participation as defined in the scoring guide.
- For a grade of F you have demonstrated no proficiency in any project and meet less than half of the expectations for participation as defined in the scoring guide.

What Do I Have to Post?

Generally one initial posting for each discussion item is a substantive posting. This is a posting that integrates the relevant reading assignments and offers a thoughtful response to the discussion question. This posting is generally longer than other postings you make. In my posting of the questions, I will make it clear whether it requires a substantive response. All material taken from the text or other resources should be cited following APA style. Please reply to at least one other post for each discussion item. Thus it becomes important to be in the course site a number of times a week so that you can take part in the discussion.

Please use the same etiquette in this class as you would in face-to-face meetings. While educated people are free to disagree with one another, do not criticize, harass, or otherwise insult other learners. Such behavior will not be tolerated. Diversity of backgrounds and experience is one of the great strengths of online education and respect for such should be an integral part of your education and learning. I expect that we will all adhere to the Academic Integrity Policy for all postings and written assignments.

Please know that the postings you make in this course may be viewed by administrators or faculty.

What Happens if I Am Going to Miss Some Time?

If you are going to be away from your computer for an extended period of time, you should make arrangements to have access to a computer while you are away. If your job or other responsibilities require that you travel, you must make arrangements to stay connected during the time you are away from your home/office computer. A connected computer is your lifeline to the classroom, so plan ahead. If you miss class because of a significant accident, severe injury or illness, or other calamity or significant disruption in your life, you should contact me as soon as possible to discuss the situation. If the disruption is predictable or recurring, like a scheduled medical exam or procedure, you must contact me prior to the time of the scheduled event.

What Can I Expect From the Course Facilitator?

I will post all discussion questions on Sunday and Tuesday. I intend to be in the course Monday through Friday and often on Sunday. I will read every posting to our classroom; however, I will not respond to all postings. If you have questions about your posts, please e-mail me. Generally my responses will be within 24 hours but may be as long as 72 hours. I will not reply to anything posted from Friday afternoon to Sunday evening until Monday. I will grade assignments in a like manner. Remember to review the discussion rubric to understand what is expected in posts.

In facilitating online learning, instructors strive for a delicate balance between challenge and support. Course content and activities must provide optimal challenge to keep learners curious, interested, and motivated to learn. It is necessary to balance this challenge with adequate support through a network that may include the instructor, peers, the technology team, university resources, student services, the library staff, and others. Too much tilt on either side of the challenge scale without corresponding support can overwhelm learners or bore them. In either case facilitators risk lowering satisfaction with the course content as well as perceptions of learning or knowledge gained.

How Can I Get in Touch With the Faculty Member?

Please feel free to send me a mail message in the classroom using the icon that looks like an envelope on the home page. This mail program works in a similar fashion to other mail programs. This mail is forwarded to me so I will get it in my regular mailbox even if I am not in the classroom.

Tips:

- It is important to remain current in your readings and postings.
- As you post, consider changing the subject so that it is more meaningful.
- Use APA style for all posts and citations.

I look forward to working with you in this course!

How to Develop a Scavenger Hunt

The following describes how a beginning online instructor organized a scavenger hunt.

I use a scavenger hunt to make sure the students can handle all aspects of the course. The process is structured using conditional release of content. The students need to perform various tasks, and the completion of one triggers the availability of the next.

In the beginning, students need to find the course syllabus in the Content area, and they find the first clue in the syllabus. The clue tells them what to do next and ensures that they have read the syllabus! They learn from the first clue that they need to complete the course policy quiz and earn 100% before they can proceed. This means they have to spend some more time with the syllabus.

The perfect score on the quiz triggers the appearance of a news item with the next clue (I had my students upload a photo to the dropbox). The students are then informed that it might take 24 hours for the next clue. During this time, the instructor gives them feedback. A news item directs the students to read the feedback, which includes the next clue. Reading the feedback activates a news item that tells the students to post a message on the discussion board.

In my class, the discussion board posting activated the next news item with directions to watch a video about academic misconduct. Finally, I checked reports to see whether the students went to the link and stayed there for six minutes. If so, they completed the process. If not, I sent an e-mail to those students who did not spend adequate time watching the video. I was surprised by how smoothly it all went.

Tool Kit for Online Instructors

Our previous learners share practices and tools their groups considered to be most important in teaching an online course. Working in small groups, they developed the following guidance for online instructors based on our joint exploration of practices and tools. We provide a portion of their ideas and recommendations for an online teaching and learning tool kit with their permission.

Setting Expectations

Developed by Sharon Lyon-Paul, Julie Robinson, Chuck Stickelman, and Jessica Wells.

Setting expectations is an effective tool for face-to-face and online courses. Creating a learning environment that promotes motivated and engaged learners can be challenging, and the lack of face-to-face meetings that is typical of online classes can increase those challenges. As an icebreaker, you can share your thoughts and feelings about the course, your role in the class, and what you expect of yourself and the learners. By sharing your expectations you help the learners develop their own expectations and how to express them. Additionally, you are opening an important dialogue between yourself and the learners that actively includes them in the design of their personal learning experience.

What to Share

To cooperatively develop a shared set of expectations between you and the learners, you will need to share your expectations and then require the learners to respond with their expectations. When you and the learners are sharing expectations consider using the following categories:

Expectations for the Course

You can use this as an opportunity to paint the big picture for the course. You can refer to the course's learning objectives, as these are usually set in advance as part of the curriculum and are integral to the course's goals. The learners are going to use these expectations to tell you why they are in the course and what they expect to get out of it.

Expectations for the Instructor
You can use this space to outline how you see your role in the course, clearly identifying how you intend to participate in the course. The learners are going to tell you what they expect and want from you.

Expectations for the Learners
This is big! Do not skimp on the details in this section. You will find that many of your expectations are common from one course to another. That's okay. The learners will respond to your lead.

How to Share

There are several tools and methods that you can use to begin an expectations dialogue with the learners that can be combined as desired.

Telephone: You can call each learner and begin discussing expectations with them then, or you can use the call as an opportunity to direct the learners to e-mail or the course management system (CMS) such as Canvas, Blackboard, or Moodle.

E-mail: The initial contact with the learners can be via e-mail. This is a great opportunity to share your expectations and then solicit e-mail replies. The e-mail can also direct the learners to the CMS.

CMS: The CMS is the core of many online courses. Using this tool to communicate expectations is a natural. Most CMS solutions include the ability to support surveys and discussion forums. Creating a survey that asks the learners to identify all three sets of expectations can be effective. The discussion forum can be used to discuss the results of the survey and cooperatively develop a shared set of expectations.

Fostering a Community of Inquiry

Developed by Laura Bockbrader, Tiffany Halsell, Jacquelyn Lewis, and Kelsie Soneson.

A community of inquiry (COI) is a distance educational model based on three elements of collaborative learning: teaching presence, social presence, and cognitive presence. Each of these three elements works in tandem to help create a community where instructors and students share ideas, discoveries, and experiences to create a meaningful learning experience.

Why is it important to understand the COI model? The COI model provides a means for students to use higher-order thinking skills to negotiate new understandings of content while challenging preconceived unsupported positions; Garrison (2011) cites work by Lipman to explain the importance of COI. Students are more likely to participate in discussions when they feel welcome as a part of the group. This leads to higher grades and more in-depth interactions during the course. The following are the elements of COI:

- *Social presence* is the ability of participants to identify with a group, communicate purposefully in a trusting environment, and develop personal and affective relationships progressively by way of projecting their individual personalities.
- *Cognitive presence* is the extent to which learners are able to construct and confirm meaning through sustained reflection and discourse in a critical COI.
- *Teaching presence* is the design, facilitation, and direction of cognitive and social processes for the purpose of realizing personally meaningful and educationally worthwhile learning outcomes.

Using COI Elements in a Course

- Design the course with clear expectations, guidelines, and appropriate use of technology.
- Structure activities and assignments to build collaboration and comfort among students.
- Respond to students' posts and e-mails according to guidelines established at the onset of the course.
- Create a welcoming environment, which encourages and supports students.
- Allow thoughtful and meaningful exploration of course content by students through use of guided discussions and group assignments.
- Establish clear evaluations and assessments for assignments, which align with stated objectives.
- Know when to be the sage on the stage or the guide on the side.

Selecting Appropriate Activities

Developed by Garren Cabral, Blythe Jones, Lindsey Luther, Caitlyn Riederer, and Marissa Stewart.

As an online instructor, you may wonder what types of activities you can use in an online environment to make sure students are engaged and learning at the same level as in a traditional classroom environment. Luckily, technology gives us many options, and it is easier than you might think to create equivalent activities in an online course. Here are some great ideas that work well in an online classroom.

Introductions

As a part of creating social presence and teaching presence, encourage your students to make introductions at the beginning of the course, and introduce yourself as well. On the discussion board, you can guide the introductions with questions similar to ones you might use in a traditional classroom. Ask students about their background and their expectations for the course. Encourage students to post a picture. Ask your students how they prefer to learn. Finally, throw in some fun questions to create a social atmosphere and help people get to know each other!

Reflective Activities

The class discussion board is a great place to encourage reflection and critical thinking. There are a variety of prompts that you can use to get students to integrate course content. One option is to use a case study and ask guiding questions to allow students to apply what they have learned in the course. Another idea that is often successful is to have a debate in which students are assigned a position to defend. Discussion board activities are useful because they allow students to interact with content as well as with each other, increasing social presence and cognitive presence. Be creative and you can come up with a variety of discussion activities that suit the goals of the course.

Guest Speakers

With advances in technology, it's easier than ever to incorporate videos into your online course. One great application of videos is to have guest speakers. If there is someone who has extensive knowledge in the subject of the course, or someone who has an interesting perspective, you can film the interview and post the video on the course site. To make it even more interactive, you can collect questions from the students before you do the interview. Videos provide a great alternative to the text-based activities that usually dominate online discussion spaces.

Wiki Spaces

Wiki spaces are areas where multiple parties can contribute to one document. In a CMS, the instructor can track who contributes to the wiki and who edits the document. This allows you to assess participation through multiple drafts of a document, and see who contributes to different areas. One excellent use of a wiki is to encourage students to post links to current events and applications that they have noticed in the real world. For example, in a science class, students could post a link to a magazine article that relates to what they have learned in class. It is a great opportunity for students to practice application of course content, and it enhances social and cognitive presence by allowing students to interact with the material and with each other. Respond to students' wiki posts with your own ideas to further the discussion.

Managing Behavior Problems

Developed by Caryn Filson, Laura Kohlhorst-Jones, Jamie McConnell, Jamie Seger, and Heather Usher.

Behavior issues that prove to be challenging for the instructor may arise in online classrooms. Instructors should deal with issues as soon as they arise to prevent the behavior from escalating and affecting the learning outcomes of other students.

Behavior Problem: Talkers

These students like to hear themselves talk. They spend their energy making noise, often raising unnecessary issues. They may create new threads of discussion or make comments that could fit into existing threads. These students thrive on personal attention, especially from the instructor.

Solution: The instructor can ask the student to reply to existing conversations rather than starting new ones. A personal e-mail with specific suggestions to get the student back on track can help the situation. Set an example of behavior you want to see and remind students of proper protocol for the course. Be gentle with this student; he or she may be your saving grace when you need someone to participate without prodding.

Behavior Problem: Shy or Quiet Students

These students do not post on discussions or threads. They are difficult to read in an online setting because of the absence of body language (nodding of the head, etc.). You see little interaction or engagement from this student.

Solution: These students can be urged to participate more by sending them a private e-mail. The student may be having technical problems, so ask if you can help overcome any issues he or she may have. Get to know something about the student that you can use to engage him or her into a discussion later. If you have the proper software to track the student's online log time, check to see if the student could be logging on and reading other comments and learning more passively rather than actively.

Behavior Problem: Disruptive Students

These students attempt to take over the class. They may address questions or comments made toward others, including the instructor. They may use foul language, be rude, be abusive, or even be threatening to other students.

Solution: To help avoid these situations, instructors can post codes of conduct at the beginning of the course to set guidelines. To deal with a disruptive student, instructors should act quickly to prevent the behavior from escalating. The professor should file all documentation of the student's behavior and address the student privately. Instructors should reassert their authority and ensure students understand expectations. If the student becomes too unmanageable, notifying proper authorities or technical personnel could be a solution.

Behavior Problem: Overachievers

These students make it known from the get-go that they have to get an A in the course. These students may exaggerate their achievements or claim credentials they do not possess. These students may question grading on assignments or challenge your grading system. Some of these students may try to harass you into giving them an A.

Solution: Acknowledging the motivation these students have can help alleviate the intensity of their behavior. Convey to the students that the class will be rigorous and as the instructor you have established the grading criteria and requirements. Let the students know that they must work hard to earn their grade, as grades will not be awarded without being earned. Keep all correspondence with these students and choose wording wisely in e-mails or discussions. It is likely that these students are also keeping a record of your conversations, which could be used against you at a later time.

Building the Online Classroom

Developed by Naomi Adaniya, Brent Grilliot, Brenda Kraner, Regina Mosier, and Ella Smith.

Regardless of the format an instructor opts to use in his or her teaching (blended or hybrid, virtual or physical environment, asynchronous or synchronous), the online virtual classroom has the power to greatly complement and facilitate learning. As the opportunities for online education have grown, instructors have many more tools at their disposal; however, as the number of tools increases, instructors will need to know which ones are worth including.

Although this may be your first opportunity to teach online, rest assured that online education has now become much more commonplace, and, consequently, instructors are far more supported. You will not have to start from scratch. As online education has evolved, relevant software has too, and your home institution may already be providing supportive resources for online instructors (Ko & Rossen, 2010). In addition, "There is no prototypical experience of teaching online," so you have the flexibility to design your online classroom to what works best for you (Ko & Rossen, 2010, p. 8).

Although your online classroom can be designed however you wish, here are some general guidelines to follow that have been developed by experts in this field:

Space

Don't be afraid to use online space. Create or make use of a space for every activity you devise (Ko & Rossen, 2010). At the beginning of the class, you can have a syllabus area, designate an announcement and grading area, and open access to the first lesson or class. By allocating a separate area for each activity, you instantly have more control over the timing of student access and pacing. It allows you to guide students' learning better (Garrison, 2011).

Discussion Boards

Using discussion boards is fairly common in online classes because it allows students to interact with one another and gives students an opportunity to reflect on the lesson, which is one of the strengths of the online learning environment. Familiarize yourself with this tool, its structure and user options, and determine how you want you and your students to view and sort messages.

Other Tools

Teaching moments and interactions with students are definitely not limited to discussion board instruction. In fact, it is recommended that you rely on more than one form of graded assignment, so plan on using other tools (Ko & Rossen, 2010). However, do not introduce tools until you are familiar with them and have determined that they are worth the effort.

Chat rooms and whiteboards. These tools allow students to interact in real-time and even make presentations to all their classmates or a smaller group. Adobe Connect, Wimba LiveClassroom, and DimDim are examples of software that provide this sort of tool.

Group sharing. Tools that facilitate group interactions allow students to gain more from group class work. This can be done as simply as opening a group discussion board, or you can use additional online software like Ning, a sort of social networking site that allows blogs and uploading files. Wiki software may be better as it provides any instructor with the ability to see a page history.

Quizzes and tests. Many of the classroom management software programs colleges and universities have purchased or developed already have the tools to allow instructors to design and post online quizzes. However, if you do not have the tool, the following are some online quiz-building resources: SurveyMonkey.com, ProProfs.com, and EasyTestMaker.com

Voice or audio messages. This can be done through a basic MP3 recorded digitally or through a podcast. Another example is the program VoiceThread, which allows students to draw on an image (or document) and leave a voice message called a *doodle*. Effective audio messages need to be very clear, so you may need to purchase a higher quality microphone and download a recording and editing program, such as Audacity. A simpler way to include audio messages may be through PowerPoint, which allows embedding audio files.

Web 2.0. If you are considering Web 2.0 tools, note that these tools are continually in development. You will need to keep up with these changes, and before you introduce them to your online classroom, consider the tool's availability, time necessary for students to learn the software, overall ease of use, and purpose. The tools included in Web 2.0 are the following:

- Social networking: Facebook
- Virtual worlds: Active Worlds, Second Life
- Avatars: Voki
- Animated movies: DoInk, Digitalfilms

Determining Value
Although some of the additional tools listed here or found online do add to the online classroom, it can be overwhelming for instructors to learn about all the available tools. Online instructors need to determine quickly which tools are worth the effort and which ones are not. Ko & Rossen (2010) offer a helpful list of rules to follow as you determine when to use and not use multimedia tools (see pp. 278–282).

Helpful Links
The following are several useful websites you can access to introduce the various software and tools available to you when teaching in an online classroom:

- EduTools: www.edutools.info/course
- Ohio Learns: www.estudentservices.org/ohiolearns
- Sloan Consortium: sloanconsortium.org

REFERENCES

Allen, I. E., Seaman, J., Poulin, R., & Straut, T. T. (2016). *Online report card: Tracking online education in the United States.* Retrieved from http://onlinelearningsurvey .com/reports/onlinereportcard.pdf

Anderson, L. W., & Krathwohl, D. R. (Eds.). (2001). *A taxonomy for learning, teaching, and assessing: A revision of Bloom's taxonomy of educational objectives.* New York, NY: Longman.

Anderson, T. (2003). Getting the mix right again: An updated and theoretical rationale for interaction. *International Review of Research in Open and Distance Learning, 4*(2). Retrieved from www.irrodl.org/index.php/irrodl/article/view/149/230

Anderson, T., Rourke, L., Archer, W., & Garrison, R. (2001). Assessing teaching presence in computer conferencing transcripts. *Journal of Asynchronous Learning Networks, 5*(2), 1–17.

Barbe, W. B., Swassing, R. H., & Milone, M. N. (1979). *Teaching through modality strengths: Concepts and practices.* Columbus, OH: Zaner-Bloser.

Bereiter, C. (1994). Implications of postmodernism for science, or, science as progressive discourse. *Educational Psychologist, 29*(1), 3–12.

Boettcher, J., & Conrad, M. (2016). *The online teaching survival guide: Simple and practical pedagogical tips* (2nd ed.). San Francisco, CA: Jossey-Bass.

Brookfield, S. (2011). *Teaching for critical thinking: Tools and techniques to help students question their assumptions.* San Francisco, CA: Jossey-Bass.

Brookfield, S. D., & Preskill, S. (2005). *Discussion as a way of teaching: Tools and techniques for democratic classrooms* (2nd ed.). San Francisco, CA: Jossey-Bass.

Brunk-Chavez, B., & Miller, S. J. (2007). Decentered, disconnected, and digitized: The importance of shared space. *Kairos, 11*(2). Retrieved from english.ttu.edu/ Kairos/11.2/binder.html?topoi/brunk-miller/index.html

Chen, F.-C., & Wang, T. C. (2009). Social conversation and effective discussion in online group learning. *Educational Technology Research and Development, 57,* 587–612. doi:10.1007/s11423-009-9121-1

Danesh, A., Bailey, A., & Whisenand, T. (2015). Technology and instructor-interface interaction in distance education. *International Journal of Business and Social Science, 6*(2), 39–47.

Dennen, V. P. (2008). Looking for evidence of learning: Assessment and analysis methods for online discourse. *Computers in Human Behavior, 24*(2), 205–219.

Family Educational Rights and Privacy Act, 20 U.S.C. § 1232 (1974).

Felder, R. M., & Brent, R. (2005). Understanding student differences. *Journal of Engineering Education, 94*(1), 57–72.

Fish, W. W., & Wickersham, L. E. (2009). Best practices for online instructors: Reminders. *Quarterly Review of Distance Education, 10*(3), 279–284.

Garrison, D. R. (2011). *e-Learning in the 21st century: A community of inquiry framework for research and practice.* New York, NY: Routledge.

Garrison, D. R., Anderson, T., & Archer, W. (2000). Critical inquiry in a text-based environment: Computer conferencing in higher education. *The Internet and Higher Education, 2*(2/3), 87–105.

Glassman, M. (2016). *Educational psychology and the Internet.* New York, NY: Cambridge University Press.

Grasha, A. F. (1994). A matter of style: The teacher as expert, formal authority, personal model, facilitator, and delegator. *College Teaching, 42*(4), 142–149.

Grasha, A. (1996). *Teaching with style: A practical guide to enhancing learning by understanding teaching and learning styles.* Pittsburgh, PA: Alliance.

Hakkarainen, K. (2004). Pursuit of explanation within a computer-supported classroom. *International Journal of Science Education, 26*(8), 979–996.

Hillison, H., Pacini, C., & Williams, P. F. (2000). Confidentiality of student records in the electronic frontier: Professors' and administrators' obligations. *Journal of Accounting Education, 18*(4), 301–313.

International Board of Standards for Training, Performance, and Instruction. (2010). *Instructor competencies.* Retrieved from ibstpi.org/download-center-free

Kearsley, G., & Shneiderman, B. (1998). Engagement theory: A framework for technology-based teaching and learning. *Educational Technology, 38*(5), 20–23.

Ko, S., & Rossen, S. (2010). *Teaching online: A practical guide* (3rd ed.). New York, NY: Routledge.

Kreber, C. (2011) Empowering the scholarship of teaching and learning: An Arendtian and critical perspective. *Studies in Higher Education, 38*(8), 1–13.

Langer, E. J. (1997). *The power of mindful learning.* New York, NY: Addison.

Lee, J- L., & Hirumi, A. (2004). *Analysis of essential skills and knowledge for teaching online.* Retrieved from ERIC database. (ED485021)

Leinonen, T., & Kligyte, G. (2002). *Future learning environment for collaborative knowledge building and design.* Paper presented at the Second International Conference on Open Collaborative Design for Sustainable Innovation, Bangalore, India. Retrieved from www2.uiah.fi/~tleinone/leinonen_fle3_os.pdf

Levine, S. J. (2007). *Getting to the core: Reflections on teaching and learning.* Raleigh, NC: Lulu Press.

Lipponen, L. (2000). Towards knowledge building: From facts to explanations in primary students' computer mediated discourse. *Learning Environments Research, 3*, 179–199.

Lock, J. V., (2002). Laying the groundwork for the development of learning communities within online courses. *Quarterly Review of Distance Education, 3*(4), 395–408.

McConnell, D. (2006). *s-Learning groups and communities.* Maidenhead, Berkshire, England: Open University Press.

Mezirow, J. (1991). *Transformative dimensions of adult learning.* San Francisco, CA: Jossey-Bass.

Nandi, D., Hamilton, M., & Harland, J. (2012). Evaluating the quality of inter-action in asynchronous discussion forums in fully online courses. *Distance Education, 33*(1), 5–30.

National Center for Education Statistics. (2016). *Employees in degree-granting post-secondary institutions, by employment status, sex, control and level of institution, and primary occupation: Fall 2013* [Table 314.30]. Retrieved from https://nces.ed.gov/programs/digest/d14/tables/dt14_314.30.asp?referrer=report

Padilla Rodriguez, B. C., & Armellini, A. (2013). Student engagement with con-tent-based learning design. *Research in Learning Technology, 21*(1). Retrieved from http://www.researchinlearningtechnology.net/index.php/rlt/article/view/22106

Palloff, R., & Pratt, K. (2011) *The excellent online instructor: Strategies for professional development.* San Francisco, CA: Jossey- Bass.

Palloff, R., & Pratt, K. (2013). *Lessons from the cyberspace classroom: The realities of online teaching* (2nd ed.). San Francisco, CA: Jossey-Bass.

Rheingold, H. (2000). *The virtual community: Homesteading on the electronic frontier* (2nd ed.). Cambridge, MA: MIT Press.

Riechmann, S. W., & Grasha, A. F. (1974). A rational approach to developing and assessing the construct validity of a student learning style scales instrument. *Journal of Psychology, 87*(2), 213–223.

Schellens, T., & Valcke, M. (2006). Fostering knowledge construction in univer-sity students through asynchronous discussion groups. *Computers & Education, 46*(4), 349–370.

Smyth, R. (2011). Enhancing learner-learner interaction using video communica-tions in higher education: Implications from theorizing about a new model. *British Journal of Educational Technology, 42*(1). Retrieved from dx.doi.org/10.1111/j.1467-8535.2009.00990.x

Stavredes, T. (2011). *Effective online teaching: Foundations and strategies for student success.* San Francisco, CA: Jossey-Bass.

Stein, D. S., & Wanstreet, C. E. (2011). Teaching in the future: A blueprint for faculty development. In S. D'Agustino (Ed.), *Adaptation, resistance and access to instructional technologies: Assessing future trends in education* (pp. 445–459). Hershey, PA: IGI Global.

Stein, D. S., & Wanstreet, C. E. (2013). Coaching for cognitive presence: A model for enhancing online discussions. In Z. Akyol & D. R. Garrison (Eds.), *Educational communities of inquiry: Theoretical framework, research and practice* (pp. 133–147). Hershey, PA: IGI Global.

Stein, D. S., & Wanstreet, C. E. (2015). Discussions in online and blended learn-ing: A tool for peer assessment. In S. Koc, X. Liu, & P. Wachira (Eds.), *Assessment in online and blended learning environments* (pp. 253–267). Charlotte, NC: Information Age.

Stein, D. S., Wanstreet, C. E., & Glazer, H. R. (2011). Knowledge building online: The promise and the process. In V. C. X. Wang (Ed.), *Encyclopedia of information communication technologies and adult education integration* (pp. 985–998). Hershey, PA: IGI Global.

Stein, D. S., Wanstreet, C. E., Glazer, H. R., Engle, C. E., Harris, R. A., Johnston, S. M., . . . Trinko, L. A. (2007). Creating shared understanding through chats in a community of inquiry. *Internet and Higher Education, 10*(2), 103–115.

Zang, J., & Walls, R. (2009). Instructors' self-perceived pedagogical principle implementation in the online environment. In A. Orellana, T. Hudgins, & M. Simonson (Eds.), *The perfect online course: Best practices for designing and teaching* (pp. 87–106).Charlotte, NC: Information Age.

Zimmerman, T. D. (2012). Exploring learner to content interaction as a success factor in online courses. *International Review of Research in Open and Distributed Learning, 13*(4). Retrieved from www.irrodl.org/index.php/irrodl/article/view/1302

ABOUT THE AUTHORS

David S. Stein is an associate professor in the College of Education and Human Ecology at The Ohio State University. He received his Ph.D. in adult education from the University of Michigan. He specializes in faculty preparation and adult teaching and learning in online environments. He has consulted internationally on technology and adult education, has written extensively on how adults learn, and has been recognized for excellence in research by the American Association for Adult and Continuing Education and for teaching excellence by University of Wisconsin Extension.

Constance E. Wanstreet is an instructional designer at Franklin University, Columbus, Ohio. She teaches instructional design and adult learning theory at Franklin and The Ohio State University. She received her Ph.D. in workforce development and education from Ohio State and has presented at international and national conferences, primarily on how adults learn in online environments. She has been recognized for instructional design innovation by the National University Technology Network and for teaching excellence by Franklin University.

INDEX

rhythms of, 52
space concerns, 25–27
style clusters, 33–34
teaching presence and, 66
open-source materials, 27–28
outcomes element. *See also*
    assessment
    assessment challenge related to,
    5, 16
    completion plan and, 7
overachievers, 140
Overview tab, 58

Palloff, R., 54
participants element, 3
    challenges related to, 5
    completion plan and, 6
participation
    Four Rs for, 79
    importance of, 77–78
    knowledge building and group
        readiness for, 110
    monitoring, 86–87
    monitoring interaction and,
        81–83
    schedule for discussion, 80
    small-group and whole-group
        activities, 80
    teaching presence through
        promoting, 79–80
people person, 37
performance areas, in transition to
    online teaching, 15–16
performance improvement, using
    feedback for, 96–97
persona, 34
    development and changes in,
        32–33
    establishing online, 44–45
    style and character clusters, 33
personal feedback, 83

personalities
    online classroom and, 26
    of online instructor, 17
philosophy, online teaching, 20, 21
platforms, online. *See* online
    instructional platforms
podcasts, 52, 127–28
polls, surveys, and quizzes, 128
postings
    discussion participation schedule
        and, 80
    responding to group, 61
    time for responding to, 38, 39
    weekly grade, 99
PowerPoint, 28, 52, 57
Pratt, K., 54
presence. *See also* social presence;
    teaching presence
    cognitive, 66, 78, 94, 137
    online instructor, 38–41
    predictability, 40–41
privacy, 84, 98
private communication, 41
procedural feedback, 96

questionnaires
    beginning online instructor
        competencies, 115–17
    online teaching attitude, 119
quiet students, 139
quizzes, 128
    software, 141–42

reactions, tools for classroom,
    97–98
readings
    in suggested course plan, 29
    tab, 58
Recorder role, 86
reflection. *See also* learner-self
    interaction

Also available from Stylus

The Blended Course Design Workbook
A Practical Guide
Kathryn E. Linder

The Blended Course Design Workbook meets the need for a user-friendly resource that provides faculty and administrators with instructions, activities, tools, templates, and deadlines to guide them through the process of revising their traditional face-to-face course into a blended format.

Providing a step-by-step course design process that emphasizes active learning and student engagement, this book will help instructors adapt traditional face-to-face courses to a blended environment by guiding them through the development of course goals and learning objectives, assignments, assessments, and student support mechanisms with technology integration in mind. It will also help instructors choose the right technologies based on an instructor's comfort level with technology and his or her specific pedagogical needs. The book will help each instructor who uses the text to develop a unique course by making choices about course design based on student learning needs for the instructor's chosen topic and discipline. Every component of the workbook has been piloted with faculty designing and implementing blended courses and then revised to better meet the needs of faculty across a range of comfort levels with technology use.

"*The Blended Course Design Workbook* brings together the best practices in online learning and residential teaching in a single concise volume and provides a wealth of resources, checklists, and step-by-step instructions essential for the development and teaching of cutting-edge college courses."—*Joshua Kim, Director of Digital Learning Initiatives, Dartmouth Center for the Advancement of Learning (DCAL)*

"The perfect mix of theory and practice, this book equips you to teach your first blended course, redesign an existing class to be more effective, or even launch an entire blended program at your institution."—***Bonni Stachowiak**, Associate Professor of Business and Management, Vanguard University; and host of the* Teaching in Higher Ed *podcast*

22883 Quicksilver Drive
Sterling, VA 20166-2102

Subscribe to our e-mail alerts: www.Styluspub.com